FORTRESSES

An Airman's Story of Survival

To Thomas

by Thomas Glide

Enjoy!

Harbor Beach. Michigan

ISBN: 978-0-615-615318

Cover and text design by Rose Island Bookworks

Printed in the United States

Dedication

To this book's biggest fan, my sister Kathy, who has a wonderful ability to unearth the most obscure facts, and keep her little brother inspired to keep working at it until it was done. (No, WE did it Kath!)

Acknowledgments

To the members of the Huron Area Writers Group for all of your help, encouragement, ideas, and motivation to turn a good idea into a great book. Without all of you, I've no doubt this would still be a handful of chapters in a box under the bed.

To all members of all branches of the military, past and present, as well as their families, for making the ultimate sacrifice, so that we can enjoy the freedoms we all have.

A special thanks to the families of Veterans, past and present, who 'gave all', especially Al, Anne, and Paul Backus. Rest in peace PFC Brian Backus.

Contents

Introduction

An old black and white 8x10 photo of eight young soldiers standing in front of a big airplane hung in our living room for as long as I could remember. The date stamped in the lower left corner read July 27, 1944.

When I was five years old, I asked my mom who those people were, and why we had a picture of them.

"That's your father in the back row, second from the left," she told me. "The rest were some very good friends of his."

I thought he looked like my older brother, not my dad.

On July 28th, 2010, sixty-six years and one day after that picture had been taken, I found myself standing on the tarmac at Willow Run Airport, staring up at a beautifully restored B-17 named The Yankee Lady.

Seven other lucky men and I were about to embark on a journey that would take about forty-five minutes, but it would take us to another place in time. As odd as it may seem, it felt more like I was completing this journey rather than starting it. But, I'm getting ahead of myself.

When I got a little older, I learned that the plane in the picture was also a B-17. Dad and the others flew in it during World War Two. I vaguely remembered hearing something about the war in history class. I also learned Dad was a prisoner of war for eight and a half months.

"Oh, ya mean like Hogan's Heroes?" I asked.

"Well, sort of." He told me.

How cool was that!? I wanted to know more. What was it like? Did you fly the plane? How come I've never seen or met these guys in the picture? Which one is Mike Postek? (a friend that Dad often spoke of) What was being a prisoner of war like? Did you meet Sergeant Schultz?!

I had a million questions, but Dad was a busy guy. He rarely spoke of his experiences, and the few stories he did tell sounded glamorous. He was the radio operator on that plane. He had seen a lot of the world and had a lot of fun in his day. Despite not being a member of his crew in the picture, Mike seemed to be a big part of his life somehow.

Before I knew it, I was becoming a young man myself. I became less interested in stories about his life because I was busy making one of my own. When I came of age, the recruiters that haunted my graduating class made a pretty good case for the military. I considered following in dad's footsteps, so I told him about the "deal" they were offering me.

"If you take it, I'll break both of your legs!" was Dad's response.

Cars were my real passion anyway, but I wondered why he felt that way. Dad could be mysterious in regard to his time in the military, and would only give me pieces of the puzzle that was a huge part of his life. The pieces came to me on his terms, bit by tiny bit, and you dared not ask for more. I'm proud to say, I have all the pieces now. The sad part is, by the time I connected them together, Dad had already passed away.

The Yankee Lady literally flew into my life for the first time in the spring of 2001 as part of an airshow at our local airport. It arrived there three months after Dad flew out of my life with his own set of wings, leaving behind an old Army suitcase full of memoirs of his days as an airman.

They were offering rides in the plane that day, and I would have given anything to take one. Sadly, the cost of doing so kept my feet firmly planted on the ground. I settled for a look inside, then stood back and watched it take off without me.

Seeing it up close and in flight was what prompted me to take a closer look at Dad's memoirs, which told an amazing story of bravery, courage and heroism. A story that was far from glamorous, and not even close to Hogan's Heroes. These young men had cajones made of solid titanium. I dove headlong into the story, gaining a whole new perspective and admiration for not only Dad and his crew, but for what truly was the Greatest Generation.

It would take nine years to wind up at Willow Run, the home of The Yankee Lady, running my hands over her shiny aluminum skin, tracing the "8" in the Eighth Air Force decal on her side with the tip of my finger, and admiring her like she was a long lost friend. This time, I had a ticket for a ride.

"You're not scared to be going up in something this old?" my sister asked me moments before boarding. She and my son Jacob were responsible for giving me this surprise ride.

It was an appropriate question. I couldn't get off of most of the commercial flights that I'd taken in my life soon enough, but I couldn't have felt more at ease climbing aboard this flight. Even though it was old, this airplane was lovingly restored and had an FAA safety rating much higher than any commercial aircraft in the world. Judging from the many medals, awards and patches from skirmishes all over the world on the flight suits of the veteran pilot and co-pilot, it was obvious they weren't just tossin' the keys to just anyone with a license to fly either. They had paid a lot of dues and earned the right to fly it.

I climbed in and settled into my "position" in the radio room, just as Dad did so many years ago, and listened to the crew begin to go through the checklist, and, one by one, start the massive engines.

On September 30, 1944, Dad and his crew performed the same ritual with memories of a previous mission still etched in their minds. They had returned from that mission running on fumes, missing an engine, a large chunk of the tail section and half of the vertical stabilizer. The fuselage was heavily damaged from flak and enemy fire. It was a miracle they landed safely. Yet, here it was, a week later, and they were preparing to go back to the same place.

They sought not fame nor glory. They simply had a job to do. Suck it up, soldier. It's time to take off.

In the fall of '44, eight brave souls left England, heavily armed, heading for Germany and a highly protected target. They didn't know what would happen, or if they'd make it back. They were the ones who had every right to be scared.

On a lazy summer afternoon in 2010, The Yankee Lady and eight tourists armed with cameras gently lifted off for a short, nostalgic flight at fairly low altitude over lush farmland, small inland lakes, and beautiful scenery over rural Michigan.

On that day back in '44, Dad and his crew would fly at high altitude and ward off subzero temperatures, flak and enemy fighters over the skies of Germany. Moments after dropping their bombs, another crippled bomber would crash into Dad's plane eight feet behind where he was sitting, shearing his plane in half, catapulting him from his plane, deep into enemy territory, with a parachute in his hand. There would be only one other survivor from Dad's crew. They would helplessly watch the two tangled planes carrying the remaining six of their friends and an entire crew from the other slam into the ground and burst into flames. Dad wound up being shot in the leg and captured by the Nazi SS once he hit the ground.

I thought about the first time I was ever on an airplane. We encountered some heavy turbulence that was tossing that 747 around like it was a toy. I swore if I made it out of that plane, I'd never set foot in another one, but Dad slept through the whole thing. Small wonder. It must have been like a ride at the kiddie park, compared to what he had gone through.

I also thought of another trip dad and I took to Florida shortly after my mom passed away. It was 1985, and I finally got to meet the elusive Mike Postek.

Even at an older age, dad was a tough guy. He spoke what was on his mind, and if you didn't like it, tough shit. I never saw him back down from anything, nor do I recall ever seeing him scared of anything. He was the type to never take crap from anyone.

You could imagine my shock when I watched the two of them stand silent and stare at one another, before wrapping their arms around each other and hugging for a good five minutes. It was the first time they had seen each other in forty years, and both men were crying like babies. The three of us spent the day together and had a great time. I got a few more pieces of the puzzle which I casually filed in my memory. I have to confess, my thoughts were more on our plans to hit Daytona Beach the next day. It wouldn't be until I read Dad's memoirs that I would know Mike's story and just how much the two of them leaned on each other to make it through some horrific times in prison camp.

I wished I had known more of what they had gone through before it was too late to tell them how proud I was of them, but I understand why they chose to put it all behind them. Reading about what they and thousands of other young men went through was amazing. Living it must have been another story. They never asked what was in it for them, they did what they did for the good of the world. If you ask any veteran from that time about it, they will all tell you to this day, it was "no big deal".

All too soon, the tires of The Yankee Lady screeched to a gentle thump on the runway of Willow Run and she was taxied back to the hanger. My journey had come full circle. I had the last piece of the puzzle. Granted, the basic picture was completed in the form of this book, but the ride was that insignificant little piece off in the corner that made my puzzle complete.

The plane is a portal to a simpler time. A time when things were very tough, but working together accomplished miracles. A special time in history that not enough people know or care about. This book is based mostly on firsthand accounts of that time period from people who lived it. I hope you enjoy reading it as much as I have enjoyed bringing it back to life.

Rear from L to R: Jesus "Rocky" Rodriguez, Harold "Kid" Ortlip, John Malloy, J.J. Jupinko, Jack Glide, Thomas "TC" Bingham
Front L to R: Edwin "Gip" LaFlame, Alan Austin, Mark Levine

CHAPTER ONE

Brothers in Arms

September 30, 1944
Debach Air Base
Suffolk, England

Life sure can be complicated, I thought to myself. I shielded my lighter from the breeze and lit up a cigarette. I took a long drag, exhaled slowly, and looked up at the huge B-17 bomber in front of me.

She is a magnificent aircraft- seventy-five feet long, with wings reaching out over one hundred feet. Four huge Cyclone engines, each producing 1200 horsepower hang from the wings. She holds over two-thousand pounds of bombs in her belly and .50 caliber machine guns are mounted in front, back, both sides, and even the top and bottom of it. The Army Air Corps aptly refers to the B-17 as the Flying Fortress.

This plane is painted olive drab green and white, but looks remarkably like the shiny silver four-engine plane I saw on a recruitment poster just a few short years ago. That poster led to my escape from Detroit, a broken down Cadillac, a pretty young socialite, and her pissed off dad. It's a long story.

My name is Jack Glide. I am the radio operator and part of the crew on this plane based in Debach, England, right in the middle of World War Two.

The plane also brings up thoughts of my mom. She died when I was seven. I used to sit on her lap, look at the pictures and listen to her read stories of far off exotic places from stacks of old National Geographic magazines she kept in boxes under her bed. We'd dream of flying all around the world when in reality, we couldn't even afford to leave our hometown.

In a way, I guess I'm living her dream of seeing the world. It ain't been Fiji, but I have seen more of the world than I ever thought I would. Still, I can't wait to get back to Detroit, the very place I ran from. Another long story, another pretty girl. And all of that is just a small part of my complicated life.

I took another deep drag and looked up at the Royal Purple Heart with swept back silver wings that had been freshly painted on the nose of the plane. It appeared to be flying at high speed with neatly spaced bombs falling from and trailing behind it. In bright yellow, the words "The Purple Heart" were emblazoned under it.

"Fits the ol' bucket a bolts, don't it?" I heard from over my shoulder.

Sgt. Harold Ortlip, our flight engineer, had walked up behind me and was staring up at the nose art. Harold is from New Jersey. He is twenty-one, with a skinny build and light blond hair that make him look like he's about fifteen, so to us, he is known as "Kid".

"It sure does, Kid," I said, holding my lighter out to his cigarette.

Our plane didn't have the nose art before our last flight. That mission took us over a highly protected munitions plant in Beilefeld, Germany. By the end of it, we had been in the air for nine hours, the tail had sustained major damage, the rudder controls were nearly destroyed, and the fuselage was riddled with bullet holes. Flak and the resulting fire consumed one of the four engines and it was a crap shoot as to whether we had enough fuel to make it back to England.

Our co-pilot, Lt. Major Mark Levine, was using the remaining three engines to help steer the plane on final approach while our pilot, Lt. Edison LaFlame wrestled with the mangled controls. As LaFlame shouted over the radio to brace ourselves for a rough landing, we all heard Levine shout, "If we make it, they oughta give this old bird a Purple Heart!"

We hit the tarmac nearly sideways and so hard that we bounced like a rubber ball, twice, skidding off the runway and into the grassy field next to it. We made it, and surprisingly all of us were unhurt. She had earned her new name and art.

Today, she has been completely rebuilt and we are preparing for our fifth bombing mission to, of all places, the same damn target in Beilefeld.

None of our previous flights were what I'd call uneventful, but they did seem to get worse each time. The brass tell us we're winning and it's getting easier. Funny thing is, I don't see any of them climbing in any of these old birds.

Our waist gunner, Sgt. John Malloy, along with our tail gunner, Sgt. Jerry "J.J." Jupinko, came around the plane and joined us. They make quite a pair, Malloy being a short, stocky dark-haired kid from the Bronx chomping on his ever present cigar, and J.J. being a rail thin freckle- faced, buck-toothed redhead from Cleveland.

"Ain't dat a sight for sore eyes," Malloy said in his gravelly voice as he took the spit-soaked stogie out of his mouth and pointed it up at the nose.

"No one knows better'n ol' J.J.," we heard our ball gunner Sgt. Thomas "T.C." Bingman say as he rounded his way around the front of the plane to join us.

"Yeah, and I thought you had the worst spot sittin' in the glass house," J.J. said as he pointed to the turret under the plane.

The truth of the matter was that J.J. owed his life to a jammed machine gun on our last mission. He had crawled out of his position in the tail to find something to dislodge the jammed shell when flak destroyed the very area he had been sitting just a few heartbeats before.

"Woulda made a hell of a suppository," T.C. joked.

"Aww, I tinks ya's both Looney Toons!" Malloy barked, "Ain't nobody should be sittin' in no glass ball under an airplane or layin' down hangin' offa the tail either!"

"Hey, they said I was gonna see the world didn't they? I see the whole damn thing," T.C. said, shrugging his shoulders.

"Anybody hear how Rocky's doin'?" Malloy asked.

"Doc says it's appendicitis. Looks like he'll be doin' some bunk flyin' for awhile," Ortlip replied.

Lt. Jesus "Rocky" Rodriguez is our bombardier. He grew up on the south side of Chicago, is built like a bull, and is every bit as ornery as one. He wound up in the Air Corps by way of a choice a criminal court judge gave him. Rocky had single-handedly cleared a bar room and sent several people to the hospital. His choice was the Army or jail. The Army paid better.

"Who's takin' his place then?" Malloy asked.

Losing Rocky at the last minute left us in a pickle. If we couldn't find someone to take his place, we could be scrubbed from the mission. Another crew and plane would have to take our place. Being grounded was safer, but we all gotta go up sooner or later. If it were up to me, I'd just as soon get it the hell over with.

"Looks like we're about to find out," Ortlip said as we turned to the sound of an approaching Jeep.

Driving the Jeep was our pilot Lt. Edison "Gip" LaFlame. At six-foot-four, he was imposing in size and nature. His facial features were chiseled as though they were carved out of granite. In the Jeep, his whole head stuck out above the windshield, but his hat and hair never move. Gip was from a well-to-do family back in Allegheny County, Pennsylvania and was always brimming with self confidence, leaving no doubt as to who was in charge both on the ground and in the air. We all considered him an arrogant self-centered son of a bitch at first, but time in actual combat has proved he was just what our crew of scrappy thugs needed. He was also quickly gaining a reputation as one of the best heavy bomber pilots in the entire Eighth Air Force.

Gip got his nickname when a drunken local, a retired Merchant Marine, literally ran into him in a pub as we were coming in. After the old gent bounced off of LaFlames chest, he stood there bewildered, looked up wide-eyed at all the medals on LeFlames uniform, before quickly snapping a salute. As he fell backwards we heard him say "Aye, Aye, Gip…" He was unable to finish his slurred sentence before landing flat on his back. The name stuck and also made Gip one of the guys.

Next to him sat our co-pilot, Lt. Mark Levine, a soft spoken quiet-by-nature farm boy from Iowa who was still studying the flight plan. In the back of the Jeep was our First Officer and navigator, Alan Austin from Nebraska. As the Jeep pulled up near the plane, we recognized Lt. Vincent O'Neil, the bombardier from the Lucky Lass. He jumped out carrying the green canvas bag marked TOP SECRET that held our Norden bomb sight, a relatively new and highly sophisticated piece of equipment that allows the bombardier to steer the plane on final approach to our target.

"What the hell'r you doin' here? Didn't you do your twenty-five?" I asked as he walked past us. He had done his required 25 missions and he and his crew should have been heading stateside for a more cushy duty.

"Yeah," O'Neil said, shrugging, "But our flight home has been held up a coupla days, so I volunteered to fill in for Rocky."

"What're ya, nuts?" Malloy asked, putting a voice to what we were all thinking.

"Maybe," O'Neil chuckled as he gently placed the bomb sight inside the escape hatch in the front of the plane. "But I figger I got nuttin' to lose, seein' you guys made it back last time missin' half this damn plane. Besides, just sittin' around waitin' to get home is drivin' me nuts!"

As O'Neil boosted himself up to install the sight, LaFlame and

Levine inspected the repairs to the plane's exterior.

"What's the good word, Captain?" Malloy asked.

"They've called the war off? We're all goin' home?" J.J. asked hopefully with a wide grin on his face and his two-sizes-too-big ears sticking out of the sides of his leather hat.

"Funny, J.J., and nice try," LaFlame said. "The Brits bombed the hell out of our target last night. There should be a lot of damage already."

"How 'bout that! We finally got a milk run!" J.J. said cheerfully.

"There's no such thing as a milk run!" LaFlame warned. "I want everyone alert and ready for anything!" he added, giving us all a stern look.

"All set!" we heard O'Neil's voice echo from inside the Purple Heart.

"Let's get this old bird in the air, men," LaFlame said. "We got a package to deliver."

"Special delivery! Special delivery for the Fuehrer!" J.J. said in a mock nasal voice as he, Malloy, Bingman, and I climbed into the plane and skimmed through the narrow passageway past the rows of bombs to our positions in the back half of the plane.

"Yeah. An' I hope dey got enough postage on 'dese babies," Malloy said, tapping on a bomb as he passed through. "Sure hate to get one a 'dese tings back!"

I was feeling a little uneasy about this flight as I settled into my position in the radio room, switching the radio and intercom on. This should be a relatively safe flight—we were flying into an area that had already been heavily damaged hours ago—but you just never know. Any flight through enemy territory can go to hell in a heartbeat.

Austin made his way through the bomb bay and handed me a copy of the flight plan. We all do double duty as a precaution. In my case, I'd take over as navigator, should something happen to

Austin. All of us have logged time at the controls of some type of airplane and if it came down to it, any one of us could fly the plane if necessary.

"Looks like a shorter run today," I said, studying the flight plan and double checking the miles and coordinates that meant a much shorter, and possibly more dangerous, return flight across enemy territory. I thought about the last time we had to do that, and how LeFlame, Levine, and Austin did a great job of flying hidden in any cloud banks we could find along the way, using only instruments and a compass to navigate. It was a little unnerving not being able to see where the hell we were going, but if the Jerries can't see ya, they sure as hell can't shoot ya down.

"Yeah, we should be back a couple hours sooner this time if all goes well," Austin replied. "You okay?" he asked, noticing that I was more quiet than usual.

"Yeah, I'm okay… just got the jitters I guess."

"Ain't we all, after last time," Austin said, slapping me on the back, "At least this time we got a head start from the Brits," he added as he squeezed his way through the bomb bay and back into his position behind the cockpit.

He was right. That last mission was enough to put everyone on edge. The sound of LaFlame and Levine going over the checklist, along with Austin, O'Neil, and Ortlip settling into their positions in the front half of the plane was quickly drowned out by the sound of the fuel pumps priming the engines.

One by one, the four big radial engines coughed, sputtered to life, and settled into a steady drone of power. Levine closed the bomb bay doors and we were ready to go.

As the Purple Heart inched forward and took her place in line on the runway, I began to feel more at ease. When it was our turn, LaFlame held her back and brought the rpm's up to takeoff speed. The old bird seemed eager to fly as he released the brakes and we began to accelerate quickly. I looked at my watch as the increasing rhythm of the tires on the runway gave way to silence. I entered the time of takeoff, mission number (five), and our destination in my log book.

Just twenty more to go, I thought to myself as we continued to climb and bank to the east. As we leveled off and streaked across the English Channel, we test fired all the guns, making sure they were ready to go.

I stared out at the early morning sky. The sun was just beginning to come up, fast turning the sky brilliant shades of bright red and purple.

"Red sky in the mornin', sailors take warnin'," I mumbled to myself.

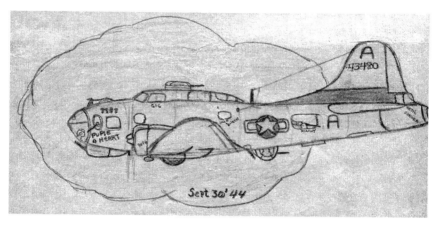

From POW Journal

CHAPTER TWO

Red Sky in the Morning

I leaned out the window and took a deep breath of cool salty sea air as I watched the English Channel go by under the right wing of the plane. A few wispy gray clouds hung in the otherwise clear, cool September sky. The air was still, and it was the perfect day for flying—for now. The red sky surely meant we would see wind and rain by evening. But, with a little luck and a tail wind, we should be back by then.

I slid back in my chair, watched the sun come up and reached inside my jacket and took a picture of my gal Eileen out of my shirt pocket. I gazed at the picture. It is of her sitting on the front lawn of her parents home back in Detroit. She is wearing a dark blue polka dot dress that fits her slender form well. Her long auburn hair is flowing down her back and she has a beautiful warm smile.

I thought of the day I got this picture back in navigator's training in Hondo, Texas. Dad had written me and told me about a young girl who wanted to start writing to me. Knowing my dad's taste in women since Mom died, I wasn't expecting much, but I sure got a surprise. Turns out she was the girl of my dreams.

She is the reason I can't wait to go back to Detroit. She has her eye on a house back home, so I have been saving every penny I can and sending it to my dad for safe keeping. I plan to surprise her when I get home.

I chuckled to myself as I remembered what my good friend Mike Postek said when he saw her picture: "Shorty, if this is your old man's taste in women, I'll take two so I can break one!"

He called me Shorty because he was a full head taller than me. He was the ONLY person I'd have let call me that. Anyone else probably would have gotten a big nose. We were the best of friends from day one of basic training, but our training eventually began to take different paths. Last I heard he had become a fighter pilot and was based in Italy.

The plane began to bank to the north, startling me back to the reality of the mission.

Looking at my compass and the flight plan, I noted the time and our position in my log book and took one last look at Eileen's picture before putting it back in my pocket.

"Mustangs at seven o'clock!" Ortlip yelled out.

I looked out the left side of the plane to see a squadron of P-51 Mustangs approaching to escort us into enemy territory. They are here because of one weakness of the Flying Fortress, speed. Our heavy plane has a top speed of around 200 mph, but the enemy fighters we are sure to encounter can reach speeds around 450 mph. The P-51's level the playing field and protect us.

"Hellooo 'dere, little buddies!" Malloy said as the fighters began to flank the bomber group. We all became silent, watching the skies closely. The arrival of support fighters was a welcome sight, but they also meant dangerous skies lay ahead of us. It wouldn't be long until we started seeing enemy fighters.

"Okay men, lets get ready," LaFlame said. "We will be approaching our target in forty-five minutes… time to take her upstairs," he added. The plane began to climb to bombing altitude and we all zipped up and donned oxygen masks.

"Let's keep it quiet, keep your eyes and ears open, and get the hell home in one piece," Levine added.

"Amen to that," I mumbled to myself as I put on my heavy lined gloves to ward off the frigid air of higher altitude. The steady drone of the engines was the only sound to be heard. Time began to crawl as we studied the sky, daring not to blink.

"We got company!" Bingman yelled out.

"I see 'em! He's comin' round the right side! C'mon Adolph! Come to Papa!" Malloy shouted and began to fire the big side gun.

A Messerschmidt 190 fighter streaked past the right side of the Purple Heart so close I could feel the turbulent air rock our plane. As it turned away, a cloud of smoke billowed out of its engine and it began to fall out of the sky.

"I got 'em!" Malloy screamed, instantly going back to scanning the sky for others. I spotted an enemy fighter coming in from behind the bomber group at the left outer edge of the formation.

"There's one at nine o'clock!" I yelled. A P-51 closed in behind the enemy fighter and opened fire. The enemy fighter burst into flames and the wreckage flew directly into another bomber, severing its left wing.

The flaming bomber fell out of formation like a rock, and began to tumble out of the sky. The crew's blood curdling screams of terror came over the radio.

"I see 'chutes... four of 'em," Bingman solemnly reported. I wrote down the coordinates and number of 'chutes. The plane fell so fast I never got a chance to see who it was.

"Looks like they got 'em on the run," Ortlip said. The remaining enemy fighters began to peel off with a group of Mustangs hot on their tails. There weren't as many enemy fighters this time. Didn't take 'em long to turn tail either. That's a good sign.

"Brace yourselves, men. We got flak straight ahead," LaFlame announced. The Purple Heart began to rock and shake as the shells began to explode all around us.

The clear sky turned dark as night with thick black sooty smoke. Shrapnel could be heard pinging and banging off of the thin aluminum skin of the plane. We continued on, weaving side to side in an effort to make us a harder target.

"We'll be at our target in five, Captain," Levine stated, pointing to the large steel roof of the munitions plant below coming into view.

"Bombardier, do you have a visual?" LaFlame asked. The flak was growing more intense.

"Affirmative, Captain, she's coming into view," O'Neil responded, readying himself for control of the plane from his position.

"Bomb bay doors open... she's all yours, O'Neil," LaFlame said lightening his grip on the steering yoke. "Line us up and drop our eggs so we can go home."

"I've got her, Captain," O'Neil said. He peered through the bomb sight and carefully steered the plane over our target. A rush of cold air blasted through the plane and the roar of the engines amplified as the bomb bay doors whirred open.

"C'mon, dammit. Drop 'em and let's go," I muttered to myself. Having to maintain a steady course with the bomb bay doors open exposes the payload to anti-aircraft fire and turns us into sitting ducks.

"Bombs away!" O'Neil yelled and threw the switch to release the bombs. The Purple Heart jumped in altitude as the enormous weight of the bombs fell from the plane. LaFlame grabbed the yoke to regain control of the plane.

"Let's get the hell outta here!" Malloy yelled. He stood ready at his side gun, staring at the sky, waiting and watching for the enemy fighters to return.

Suddenly, a huge explosion shook and rattled the Purple Heart.

"What the hell was that?" I said. I looked back at Malloy, who was staring back at me with wide eyes.

A flash of bright orange and a wave of intense heat flashed before me. There was a horrible crashing sound and then everything went dark and silent.

I awoke to a stabbing pain in my head. Frigid air was whistling past me. I could hear the engines screaming at very high rpm's. There was debris flying and circling all around me.

"What the hell," I said, struggling to regain orientation. The bright light of the blue morning sky, along with puffy white and black clouds came into focus in front of me, spinning in circles through a gaping hole of twisted and shredded metal.

"Oh shit," I mouthed to myself. I realized I was focusing on the rear half of the Purple Heart, but the only thing that was there was a hole to the open sky. Every muscle in my body tensed as I began to lift up off of the thick steel bulkhead that separated the bomb bay from the radio room that I had been lying on.

I stared in disbelief at the jagged hole to the open sky I was being pulled towards. Everything seemed silent and in slow motion. The sheer terror I had been feeling seemed to mysteriously pass. I slipped through the hole and into the open sky as the plane began to gradually fall faster than me.

I watched the tail-less plane slowly drift away from me and

flop back and forth as if it were a small leaf falling out of a tree rather than a twenty-eight ton aircraft. When it reached the ground, it slammed into a wooded area upside down in a cloud of dust. A second later, I heard the dreadful thump and explosion.

I realized I was falling from the sky, yet eerily, felt very much at ease. It was if I was watching myself go through what was happening from a safe place. Was this all a dream?

I stared up at my open parachute, but had no recollection of opening it. Parachutes! Where are the others? I scanned the sky around me, below me, and what I could see from above, but didn't see any other parachutes. Where the hell were the rest of them, dammit?

The bitter cold air rushing past me began to turn warmer. I saw the ground quickly drawing closer and a group of people gathering below me in a farm field. I heard something zing past me, and felt a deep burning pain in my left thigh. The shouting and yelling of the people below me grew louder.

When I hit the ground, I cried out in pain. My left leg felt as if it were on fire. I tumbled across the grassy knoll and came to a stop face down on the hard ground.

I rolled onto my back, closed my eyes, gritted my teeth, and reached down to my thigh. When I opened my eyes, there was a man in tattered farm clothes standing directly over me holding a pitchfork. The tines were inches from my face.

"Dont bewegung!" he yelled as a large group of civilian men and women with rifles and pitchforks began to gather around me shouting in German.

I froze in a wave of terror, not being able to understand what the man was telling me. He was trembling, and staring directly at me. He continued to wave the sharp tines in front of my face.

I could feel my heart pounding against the ground. I tried to speak, but no words would come out. I slowly tried to raise my hands above my head to surrender, noticing my left hand covered in blood. I saw a look of rage swell in the old man's eyes.

"Ich sagte dont bewegung!" he screamed, gritting his teeth and rearing back with his pitchfork.

Suddenly, three shots rang out. I jumped in fear with each one. The crowd began to scream and scatter.

As the crowd opened up, the shadow of an ominous figure appeared out of the brightness.

"Stehen Sie zuruck! Aus meinem Weg!" the figure shouted as he drew closer, blocking out the blinding sunlight. My eyes focused on the well-groomed, solidly built man. He was wearing a black and silver German S.S. Officer's uniform. Smoke wafted from the barrel of the Luger he still held pointed in the air. Two German soldiers soon flanked him, their rifles pointed at me. The officer's lapels had shiny silver S.S. insignias that resembled lightning bolts. I noticed a polished silver skull and crossbones on the front of his hat as he stood there staring right through me with icy, steel blue eyes. I had heard horror stories about Nazi officers who wore the silver skull and crossbones on their hats. They were known as "Death Heads," and were the most fanatical Nazis in the entire German army. Even their own soldiers feared them. Anyone who crossed a Death Head—friend, family, or foe—faced brutal punishment.

"Aufstehen!" one of the soldiers shouted, pointing his gun in my face. It was so close I could smell gunpowder residue. I slowly put my hands on top of my head, wincing in pain as I felt the huge bump that had formed on my scalp.

"Aufstehen!" the soldier yelled again, louder this time, and poked me in the chest with the barrel. I looked at the officer and shook my head, trying to convey to him that I didn't understand what he was saying.

"Get up," the officer said with a thick German accent. "Now!"

SEPT. 30TH '44.

From POW Journal

CHAPTER THREE

Sprechen Sie Deutsche?

Somewhere near Bielfeld, Germany

"Aufstehen!" the soldier repeated and kicked me in the side.

"Do as he says!" The officer shouted.

"I am, you sonofabitch!" I yelled, fumbling with my parachute releases. I stood up and a sharp pain shot through my leg when I put weight on it. I pressed my hand on the wound to stop the bleeding.

The officer holstered his pistol and grabbed my dog tag chain around my neck and pulled me closer. I could feel his breath on my face as he studied my tags.

"Perhaps you vould rather ve leave you to zhem?" he asked, motioning his head toward the still gathered crowd, who still had rifles and pitchforks at the ready.

"You cowards drop bombs on zhier families," he said quietly. "You kill zhier children," he added through gritted teeth and pointed to a young boy and girl in the crowd.

"I'm sure zey vould take goot care auf you, Mr. Glite," he said with an evil smile.

"Vhat kind of name is zat, Glite?" he asked as he looked up at my jet black hair.

"Are you a Jew?"

"Jack Glide, Sergeant, United States Army Air Corps, 36146317," I said, just as I had been told to, and stared straight at him.

"How do I know you are not a Jew?" The officer said as he clenched my tags in his gloved fist and stared coldly into my eyes.

I glanced down briefly at his holstered pistol. It was mere

inches from my left hand. The two soldiers stood a good distance behind him and both were looking in other directions. I thought about my injury. I only have one good leg. Would I be able to steady myself long enough to grab his gun? I can't run. I can barely stand. My eyes shifted to the still gathered crowd. Dammit.

The officer caught me glancing at his pistol and stood back a little and held his hand over it.

"You vould be vize to do as ve say… ve are here to protect you from zhem," the officer said, releasing my tags and motioning to the crowd.

"Oh yeah? Who's gonna protect me from you?" I sneered back.

"Get moving! Now!" the officer shouted, pointing towards the staff car parked on the roadside.

"I've been shot," I said. Blood was seeping through my pant leg and dripping from my fingertips.

The officer turned back to the crowd and scanned through them, stopping at an old woman. He shouted something in German at her and she took the large scarf off of her head, ran toward me and knelt in front of me. A sharp stabbing pain ran through me when she tied it tightly around my leg.

"Now get moving!" the officer shouted. The soldiers prodded me in the back with their rifles.

I began to hobble forward and felt something grinding inside my leg.

"Where are you taking me?" I asked.

"Shut up and move!" the officer shouted and gave me a shove.

I stumbled forward and fell to the ground, screaming out in pain when I landed on my wounded leg.

While I got back up and limped past the crowd of civilians toward the long, sleek, black staff car, I listened to the conversation between the soldiers and the S.S. Officer walking behind me.

"Bringen Sie ihn in den Zug in Hannover, und lassen Sie ihn

nicht anhalten." the officer told his men. The only word I understood was Hannover, the name of a town north of Beilefeld. I wished I had learned German.

"Ist er ein Juda?" one of the soldiers asked.

"Seine anhangsel sagen katholiken… but sie konnten sein imitiert," the officer answered.

What was that word Juda? Ist er something Juda, maybe Jew?

When we reached the car, the officer opened the driver's door, stood in the open doorway, and looked at me.

"Wenn er anhalt oder versucht, zu entkommen, ihn zu schieben," the officer told the soldiers.

I felt helpless. I couldn't understand much more than Hannover and possibly Jew, but it appeared the officer was giving the soldiers instructions of some sort. But for what?

"Teilen sie ihnen mit dieser soll zu Pickhardt gehen… er wird diesen genieben," the officer said. He climbed behind the wheel of the car and shut the door.

"Zhey vill take you vhere you are going," he told me, pointing to the soldiers. "Do not try to escape. Do you understand?" he said, glaring, shaking his gloved finger at me.

He gave me a stone-faced stare, started the car and put it in gear.

"Velcome to Germany! Enjoy your stay!" he told me with an evil grin. His hearty laugh faded away as the car disappeared in a cloud of road dust.

"Raush! Bekommen sie das bewegen!" One of the soldiers told me, poking me in the back with his rifle barrel and pointing down the road.

I settled into a slow, stiff-legged limp and desperately tried to block out the pain. Questions raced through my mind. I guessed they were walking me to Hannover, but how far away was that from here? What are they going to do with me once we get there? That is, if that really is where I am going. The questions about being Jewish worried me. I wondered if they believed I was Jewish, and what they would do to me.

We rounded a bend in the road and I saw a small, faded sign that read: Hannover, 16 km.

"Shit, that's ten miles," I muttered to myself. The realization of what I would likely have to do began to set in. I'm no stranger to long walks. During my childhood in the middle of the Great Depression, I used to walk everywhere. Hell, it was my only means of getting anywhere. Ten miles was nothing then. Of course, I didn't have a bullet in my leg then either.

I thought of Eileen and my family getting the news that my plane had gone down then waiting to hear if there were survivors.

I'd seen this play out all too many times back in Debach when planes went down. The returning crews would report what they had seen, what planes went down, if there were any parachutes and how many, and the coordinates at which they were last seen. I hoped someone had seen mine. We would go on record as missing and word would be sent out to our families stating only that we were missing, nothing more, nothing less. Everyone at Debach and back home would wait for news and hope for the best. The news, both good and bad, could take days, weeks, or months. Sometimes it wouldn't come at all.

And now it was happening to me. The only way anyone would know I was alive would be when I turned up somewhere.

"If it's a walk you want me to take, then let's go," I said to no one in particular.

I looked down at the scarf tied around my leg and noticed a small piece of burned flesh stuck to the front of my flight jacket. The hair on my neck stood up as I remembered the last vision I had of Malloy just before the orange flash and the heat. I stopped walking.

"Bekommen Sie das bewegen!" The soldiers shouted and jabbed me in the small of my back with their rifle barrels.

"Yeah, I know… get moving," I muttered. What a hell of a way to learn German.

Footnote: The soldiers were told his dog tags stated he was Catholic, but were probably fake. The officer then ordered them to walk him ten miles to Hannover. If he tried to stop or escape, they were to shoot him. If he made it, they were to put him on a train and send him to Pickhardt, a notoriously cruel S.S. Officer, to finish him off.

Eileen Shea

Jim and Anna Shea

CHAPTER FOUR

The Redhead Back Home

September 30, 1944
Detroit, Michigan

"Noooooo!" I heard myself shout as I leapt up in bed.

Beads of sweat were on my brow and a chill ran down my spine. I fumbled for the light switch on the lamp next to my bed. As I became more aware, memories of the horrible nightmare I had been having crept back to me.

"No! No! Nooo!," I cried out, burying my face in my hands. I began to sob.

"Good heavens, Eileen! What's wrong, dear?" My mother Anna asked, running into my room and sitting on the bed beside me.

"Something has happened," I sobbed, holding onto my mother tightly."

It's Jack. Something terrible has happened," I choked out, trying to catch my breath.

"There, there, dear. It was just a bad dream," Mom said. She held me and stroked my hair.

"But... it was so real!" I sobbed. "I was falling through the air, and... and I looked over and Jack was... " tears welled up in my eyes and my face contorted, "beside me," I squeaked out and began to sob again.

"There, there... I'm sure he is fine, dear." Mom said, holding me in her arms. "You've been working so hard... and worrying so," she reasoned, trying to console me.

"What's wrong?" my father Jim asked, entering my room still tying his robe.

"She had a bad dream. She feels something terrible has happened to Jack."

My father sat down on the bed beside me. "Miss Eileen Shea! What are we to do with you?" he asked, putting his hand over mine. "It was just a nightmare, Doll Face. It's over now."

"But Dad, it— "

"No buts!" he said, wiping the tears from my eyes with his calloused hand.

"Your mother is right. You have been working too hard with those two jobs. You're exhausted."

I have a job as a cashier at Gratiot Lumber, and had recently taken a second job as a bookkeeper at our family church. Sometimes, the Pastor would let me bring the books home, and I'd work well into the evening. I want to surprise my boyfriend Jack, who is away in England fighting in the war. When he gets back, we are going to get married and buy a home. Not just any home, but a small two-story I have loved since I was a child. It's on Radnor Street, across the street from Balduk Park, where Dad would take my sisters and me to play. I always thought the gingerbread man lived there due to the intricate hand-carved woodwork around the roof peaks and windows. There is a white picket fence and lilac bushes, my favorite, in the front yard. Jack doesn't know it yet, but I am saving every penny I can so we can buy the house when he gets back.

"You need to slow down a bit and try and get some rest." I heard Dad say.

"I have been pretty tired," I reasoned. Mom handed me a handkerchief.

"Yes, you have, dear," she said, fluffing my pillow and pulling the covers back over me when I laid back down. "Now do try and relax. I'm sure everything is just fine. You will see. Any day now you will get a letter from him telling you everything is just fine."

As they left the room, I turned and took the picture of Jack off my nightstand beside the bed. I smiled sadly.

"I wish you could just come home," I whispered, holding his picture against my heart. I smiled as I thought back to the beautiful spring day in April of 1942, when I got the picture from Jack's dad. He had moved into an apartment above the lumberyard, and while I was dusting some things off around the cash register, I heard his unmistakable voice.

"Hey, Red!" he shouted.

I turned to see him walking toward me with what appeared to be a letter and some pictures in his hands. I smiled at the sight of him. He was always good for a laugh. Loud and boisterous, he always had a smile and wore his dirty brown derby hat. He walked with a bouncy gate and called every woman he encountered Toots. Bub was reserved for every man he happened upon. He called me Red because of my long auburn hair. A lot of people didn't think much of him. To some he was nothing more than a freeloader, but to me, he was just a loveable, kindhearted man of little means with a lot of big ideas that never seemed to pan out.

"Good morning, Mr. Glide. How are you today?" I asked, expecting to hear about the latest revolutionary money-making idea he had come up with that would change the world.

"Lookie here, Red," he said as he held out the letter and pictures. "I got a letter from my boy! He's in the Army… Army Air Corps. Gonna be a fly boy, ya know… "

I chuckled. Listening to him talk was enough to cheer me, no matter what he was talking about.

"Sent us some pictures. Down in Texas, he is… in navigator's training," he said, handing the pictures to me. "Why anyone would go there is beyond me! Hotter'n the hub'sa hell there!" he explained, as if his son had a choice in the matter. "Ya know he says it's damn near a hunnert degrees there already?"

I began to look at the pictures of military barracks, tanks, airplanes and stopped at one of a very handsome young man. He was dressed in Army fatigue pants and a white t-shirt that showed his muscular arms. He had wavy, jet black hair and a beautiful smile.

"I didn't know you had a son. Is this a picture of him?"

Mr. Glide pushed his thick bifocals up the bridge of his nose and stared at the picture.

"Yep, that's my boy. Jack Jr." he said, noticing the shy smile on my face. "Whatdaya think a dem apples? Doesn't clean up to bad does he?" he asked.

"He certainly doesn't!" I said with a chuckle. "You must be very proud of him." I said. I handed the photos back and began to ring up a sale for a customer.

"Suppose I am, Red. Maybe this will make a man outta him." I heard him say in the background. "See ya, Red. You can keep this."

I finished up the sale and looked down to see the picture of his son lying on the counter beside me. I picked it up, looked at the handsome young man, and found myself smiling again.

"Hey, Red!"

I looked up to see Mr. Glide at the bottom of the staircase leading up to his apartment. He had a silly grin on his face.

"He's available too! Prolly wouldn't mind gettin' some mail from a gorgeous dame back home either!" he said, disappearing into the stairwell.

I blushed and shook my head. "You're something else Mr. Glide!" I said.

"So they tell me! So they tell me!" His voice echoed off the walls of the staircase.

I leaned over, put the picture back on the nightstand, and took one last look at the young cadet before turning off the light and falling back against my pillow.

"I sure hope you're okay, wherever you are," I sighed before slowly drifting back to sleep.

CHAPTER FIVE

This is Not the Orient Express

September 30, 1944
Hannover, Germany

"Gotta keep walking," I murmured to myself.

The sun was starting to close in on the horizon. I'd guess there is not much more than an hour or two of daylight left. My determination to reach wherever it was I'm going was starting to give way to exhaustion, hunger, and a raging thirst, none of which were effective at blocking out my throbbing headache or the searing pain in my leg. I wished I could stop, just for a moment. I looked over my shoulder at the soldiers and began to slow down.

"Bekommen Sie das bewegen! Jetzt!" one of the soldiers shouted and poked me in the back with his rifle.

I picked up my pace again. I thought of Eileen and my family getting the news and the horrible waiting game they would face.

"Gotta keep walking," I mumbled.

Missing. It sounds so open-ended, as if I were a misplaced object, like a set of keys or a pair of reading glasses. I thought of what would inevitably run through my own mind when I heard a crew had gone down, especially as more and more time passed. They are dead.

"Gotta keep walking," I continued to chant to myself.

I couldn't stop thinking about that officer asking if I was a Jew. Was he having these soldiers take me to a concentration camp? Where they making me walk to the middle of nowhere to kill me? I thought of another word the officer said that stood out among the gibberish I couldn't understand—Pickhardt—but what was that? The only thing I know for sure is that they don't want me to stop until I get there, wherever that may be. I just gotta keep walk—

"Halt!" I heard one of the soldiers shout.

I stopped and stood frozen in fear. Why were we stopping here? There's nothing here but a beaten down dirt path through a densely wooded area. This couldn't be good.

I listened to them talking and moving behind me. Their voices seemed to be calm and oddly becoming more distant—as if they were moving away from me.

I turned to face them, not knowing what to expect, hoping it wasn't going to be a belly full of lead. Instead of plotting my demise, I saw the soldiers had walked over to a nearby fallen tree trunk and were sitting down, leaning their rifles against the trunk beside them.

I collapsed in the soft grass along the road and let out a long sigh of relief. While I laid flat on my back, my whole body was aching and quivering. My gunshot wound was burning like the fires of hell. It felt good to finally rest.

I looked over at the soldiers, who had taken out a pair of canteens and were pouring cool, clean water into a pair of tin cups. They laughed as they looked at me, raising their cups and smiling before savoring each long drink.

"Bastards," rattled from my dry and dirt-filled voice box.

One of the soldiers stopped laughing and looked down at the ground. A look of pity slowly began to wash across his face as he turned to look at me. He finished his drink, then poured some more water in his cup. He walked toward me, smiling. He knelt down beside me, holding the cup out carefully with both hands.

I could almost taste the cool water as I sat up and reached out with trembling hands. When the cup was almost in my reach, the soldier tossed the water from the cup into a mud puddle next to me.

"Es gibt ihr Getrank. Schwein," he said, pointing at the puddle. His fake look of concern was replaced with contempt as he went back to his laughing cohort.

I crawled over to the puddle, skimmed some of the clean water from the top with my cupped hands and brought it up to my mouth. My lips burned, but I gulped down the warm, stagnant water. I scooped up a second helping and gulped it down, then sat there holding my wet hands over my face.

I heard voices approaching and quickly took my hands off my face. A small farm wagon being pulled by a mule was coming up the road. A German soldier was at the reins, another was walking beside it. A line of battered American soldiers and another pair of German soldiers followed closely behind it.

When the rickety wagon rattled past me, I noticed two American soldiers sitting in the back. My stomach turned when I looked at the dead body of the soldier closest to me. His uniform was badly torn and shredded. His face was burned so badly that his lips and eyelids were gone. The acrid stench of burnt flesh hung in the air. The soldier sitting up on the other side of the wagon was in much better shape. He was battered and bruised with a makeshift splint tied around his right leg. A look of astonishment came across my face when I recognized the skinny, young, blond-haired airman.

"Kid?! Is that you?" I asked.

"Jack?" Ortlip asked, staring at me in disbelief. I was wide-eyed and open mouthed, staring at him as the wagon creaked down the road.

"He made it," I muttered. "The 'lil son of a bitch made it!" I shouted.

A smile came over each of our weary faces. He was the only sign of my crew I had seen since my capture. Seeing other captured soldiers heading in the same direction as me was a good sign. It appeared we were going somewhere, even if we didn't know where.

I wondered if more of my crew survived.

"Aufstehen! Bekommen sie das bewegen!" I heard someone shout, realizing the two soldiers were now standing above me again.

I stood up and began to limp down the road again with new found energy. Seeing Ortlip gave me hope that other members of my crew might have survived as well. I looked at the faces of the other captured soldiers I had been grouped with for any more familiar faces, but found none. I kept a close eye on the wagon carrying Ortlip while we continued on. Seeing anyone brought comfort- but another crew member- well, that was a sight for sore eyes.

We crested a small hill and I could see a clearing ahead. Beyond that, there was a town in the distance. More prisoners were merging into our path, accompanied by more German soldiers. At the edge of town, I could see a small black locomotive sitting idle with smoke slowly drifting out of the stack and trailing over several red and brown boxcars behind it.

"I made it. Goddamn it, I made it," I whispered to myself as the town grew closer with each step.

I thought about the interrogation and everything I'd face next. The unknown of it all scared the hell out of me, but I didn't care. Word would be sent out that I was alive, and I knew at least one more of my crew survived as well.

When we got closer to the train, I could see more captured soldiers sitting in lines on the ground beside it. Some had their hands tied behind them. Some had their heads on their knees. All of them had that same been-through-hell look on their faces. The smell of cow manure and urine hung in the air. German soldiers were leading some cows down ramps off the train to a nearby field to graze. Other soldiers were shoveling fresh straw into empty box cars.

I kept one eye on the wagon carrying Ortlip and scanned the faces in the crowded lines of prisoners as they led me to the end of a line and ordered me to sit down. They took Ortlip off of the wagon and sat him in a line directly across from me, about thirty yards away. Sad smiles came across both of our faces as we looked at each other.

"Have you seen anyone else?" he asked me.

"Schweigen!" a nearby guard shouted, spinning around and bashing Ortlip in the side of his face with the butt of his rifle.

Ortlip fell flat on his back. The guard turned in my direction, looking for who Ortlip had been talking to. I stared at the ground.

When I looked up, Ortlip was getting back up. A huge bruise was forming on his cheek and his right eye was swelling shut. I shrugged and shook my head no. A sad look came over his face. He shook his head no as well.

"Dear God, what are they going to do with us?" A young British airman sitting next to me asked.

He was wearing an R.A.F. Captain's uniform, which, although it was dirty, still showed signs of being finely pressed at one time. I noticed his well-manicured fingernails and neatly trimmed hair while he rocked backed and forth, shuffling his feet. I sensed this was the first time he had ever been in a tight spot.

"Sure as hell ain't invitin' us for tea. Just sit still and shut the hell up." I whispered under my breath.

"I don't know if I can take this," the Brit said nervously. He buried his head in his knees, began to rock back and forth, muttering incoherently.

"Goddamn it, just sit still and, for God's sake, shut the hell up!" I whispered.

"I can't sit still!" he shouted. "They've been dragging me from place to place since the night before last. No one knows if I'm— "

"I know what you mean. But fidgetin' around ain't gonna help. It's gonna piss 'em off!"

The guards began to order prisoners at the front of the line to get up.

"Oh, dear God! This is it! Where are we going? What despicable acts are we to endure?" The young Brit's quivering voice echoed through the crowd, each word getting louder than the last.

"Calm down, dammit! You're gonna make things worse if you don't st— " I said, stopping short, noticing a guard near Ortlip look directly at us.

"Oh shit," I mumbled. The guard had started walking toward us, his eyes fixed on the young Brit next to me who was now sobbing uncontrollably with his head between his knees, heaving up and down.

"Halten Sie as auf!" The guard shouted as he approached the Brit, catching the attention of another guard at the front of the line, who started walking toward him as well.

"Ich satge Halt es! Rasch!" The second guard yelled as he approached the Brit and kicked him in the shins.

"No! No! No!" the Brit wailed, flopping around on the ground.

"Aufstehen Schwein!" the guards shouted at the Brit as they yanked him to his feet while he continued to flail around and scream for mercy.

As I and the others in our line began to walk toward the waiting boxcar, they dragged the Brit in the other direction toward a small wooded area. I looked over at Ortlip, who was being led into a box car two cars behind mine. I gave him a small wave as I began to make my way up the ramp.

A putrid odor overcame me when I got to the entrance of the box car and looked in. Dirty, trampled straw soaked in cow urine, laden with deep, slimy manure covered the entire floor. Down the line, cows were being led into the cars with the fresh new straw.

"Nooo! Please noooo!" I heard the young British soldier crying in the distance. I took one last breath of fresh air before I entered the box car, which was already crammed with fellow prisoners. Just then I heard the young Brit let out a blood curdling scream that ended abruptly with a single gunshot that echoed through the countryside and my mind.

More and more prisoners were loaded into the boxcar, and by the time the doors were shut, we were standing shoulder to shoulder, with barely enough room to move.

We all stood in the dark and stench for a few minutes before I heard someone break the eerie silence and say, "What's your name and where ya from? I'll start—Murray Stienburg... Omaha, Nebraska."

One by one more began to answer.

"Peter Weisman... Brooklyn... "

"David Cohan... Cincinnati, Ohio... "

"Paul Levy... St. Louis... "

I listened for anyone I might know, but heard nothing so far.

"Joseph Irving... Louisville, Kentucky... "

"Willie Strong," I heard a deep voice say. It sounded right behind me. "Detroit, Michigan... "

"Hey! I'm from Detroit!" I yelled out, turning as far as I could in the cramped box car to find him.

Off to my left and a couple of prisoners behind me stood the biggest, blackest man I had ever seen.

"My name is Jack... Jack Glide." I said.

The train lurched ahead and began to move down the tracks, sending most of us bouncing into each other. Willie stood there with a blank expression on his face.

"Well, we's a long ways from Detroit, Jack," he solemnly said.

How true that was. While the rest of the prisoners yelled out their names and where they were from, Detroit felt like it was a million miles away.

CHAPTER SIX

The Death Trio

October 3, 1944
Tychow, Poland

I was startled awake by the reoccurring nightmares of my last moments on the Purple Heart. With each one, more and more details were finding their way in. Some were horrible; the worst was seeing Malloy ripped from the plane by some unrecognizable object. Some just didn't make any sense. In the one I was just having, I was watching the badly damaged Purple Heart flipping through the air, and it suddenly turned upright and grew wings like a huge bird. It then silently flew away with its wings slowly flapping up and down.

The bright morning sun filtered through the slats on the side of the rail car as the train slowed and came to a stop. It was the third day I had seen the sun come up on the trip. We had stopped several times during the past few days. They would let us out to pee and sometimes we would take on supplies and water for the locomotive. Once a day, they would give us a loaf of hard, black rye bread and a bowl of saurkraut to share among the prisoners in each box car. We were all exhausted, hungry and thirsty and had taken to leaning against each other to get some rest. There really wasn't room to sit down, and no one wanted to sit in the filth on the floor anyway. As bad as prison camp sounded, I was looking forward to getting off of this train, a place to sit and some much needed medical attention. A huge knot had formed on the back of my head, and my leg stung

35

like it was covered with honeybees.

The doors were flung open on the box car, and bright sunlight washed over us.

"Kommen Sie heraus!" a guard shouted.

We all began to walk out the door and I looked at the scenery. Several German soldiers with rifles and bayonets lined the sides of the wide dirt road that led through the middle of a large stand of pine trees just outside the train. Some of the soldiers had huge German Shepard dogs on short leashes. The dogs stood at attention, looking at us. The wonderful smell of pine trees replaced the awful stench I left behind on the train. Beyond the trees and far in the distance, I could see a town. Halfway between the town and train, I could see a huge fenced in area with some large brick buildings and long wooden barracks. In the middle of the road just outside the train stood three German S.S. Officers in ominous black uniforms. The first was a fairly thin man with slicked back black hair and horn-rimmed glasses. He looked a little older than the other two, and was twitching a riding crop behind his back as he shuffled around.

The second looked to be in his mid-thirties, was a little taller and larger in build with very short black hair. He stood motionless, with a riding crop tucked under one arm, his other hand on his hip and an angry look on his face. The third was huge, had a shaved head, and stood like a silent mountain between the other two. All of them had silver skull and crossbones on their hats.

"Great. More damn Death Heads," I muttered to myself.

It appeared this wasn't just a stop; we were actually being turned over to Larry, Moe, and Curly. I breathed an uneasy sigh and joined the other prisoners from our box car who were being herded into the center of the street.

As the other box cars emptied, I noticed Ortlip standing in formation with the others from his box car. The guards were giving them more stale bread. I was happy there would be someone here from my crew and still wondered about the rest.

My heart sank though, as I watched Ortlip and the others from his box car being loaded back on the train when they finished doling out the loaves of bread. He turned and looked straight at me, giving me a nervous smile. The doors were closed behind him, and the train began to slowly pull away.

"Lassen sie diese Amerikanshchen flieger es haben!" the angry-looking officer screamed out.

All hell broke loose. The soldiers turned the dogs loose and they charged at us showing their teeth, barking and growling. The soldiers began to charge at us in a flurry of loud yells and screams, jabbing at us with their bayonets.

"Fuhren Sie Schwein!" I heard one soldier shout. In the confusion, a soldier suddenly appeared beside me, giving me a shove forward and jabbing me in the ass with his bayonet.

"Fuhren, Schwein!" He screamed.

A huge dog ran up to me and clamped his jaws on my right pant leg and began to shake it furiously.

I shook the dog loose and began to run as fast as I could. I could hear the dog growling and his teeth clicking together. Each failed attempt to get a hold of my leg was getting closer and closer. Another prisoner to the left and in front of me stumbled and fell. The dog shot out from behind me and pounced on him. A guard joined in, stabbing him with his bayonet as I ran past them. I heard the prisoner scream in agony, but I kept running as fast as I could. Another prisoner veered off of the road and tried to make a break for the wooded area. A single gunshot rang out and the prisoner fell flat on his face and lay motionless in the grass.

What the hell is going on? Those that stumbled or slowed were being savaged by dogs and bayonets. Those that tried to make a break were being shot. Gunshots repeatedly rang out behind me. I could hear the dogs barking and growling. Once in a while, I'd feel one nipping at my heels. My leg hurt like hell, but I was managing to stay ahead of the fray in the middle of the pack of confused prisoners. Staying close, and in the middle seemed to prevent the dogs and soldiers from reaching us, but those on the outside of the pack were being ripped to shreds.

I heard a whoosh and felt a stinging pain in the back of my neck. I turned and noticed the angry-looking officer running along side of me. He had an insane smile on his face and his eyes were wide open and pitch black. He looked as if he were possessed by something as he ran along and surveyed the carnage happening all around.

"Fuhren Sie Schwein!" he shouted in a high-pitched cartoonish voice as he whipped me with his riding crop and laughed wildly. "Fuhren Sie Schwein!"

CHAPTER SEVEN

The Wait Never Seems to End

October 3, 1944
Detroit, Michigan

Jim Shea lit a cigar and puffed a trio of smoke rings that drifted slowly in the calm breeze. He watched his four daughters, Eileen, Rosie, and the twins, Dot and Doe, unload the trunk of his Packard sedan. It was a beautiful Indian summer Sunday, and he decided to treat the family to a picnic at a park along the Detroit River.

He paid close attention to his oldest, Eileen. She was plodding through the grass with a picnic basket as if it were a household chore. Normally, she would be happy to be at the park—it was one of her favorite places—but she had been very quiet and sullen since the nightmare she had a few nights ago. She still hadn't heard from Jack. That wasn't unusual in war, but it sure didn't help.

"I sure hope this takes her mind off of things," he muttered.

• • •

"Feels good to be out in the fresh air, doesn't it, Eileen?" I heard my mom ask as I put the picnic basket on the table.

"Yeah," I said as I gazed out over the rippling water.

"You'll hear from him soon, dear. Everything is just fine. You'll see."

"I know mom. It's just the waiting," I said as I took a homemade apple pie out of the basket and placed it on the table.

Since Jack had gone off to war, the daily letters he would send when he was training back here in the States had trickled down to

Jack Glide Sr. and Eileen   Jack Glide Jr. and Jack Glide Sr.

L to R- Rosie, Doe, Eileen, and Dot Shea

two or three a week. Now and then, a week or two would pass before I heard anything from him. Sometimes, his letters would arrive all on the same day, making the distance between us seem even farther.

It was hard to keep my mind on anything else when I was waiting for letters from Jack. When the letters finally did arrive, I would dive into them and read and reread the stories of what it was like, thrilled he was okay, only to realize when I finished that he was still halfway around the world, in harm's way. It was an emotional roller coaster ride I was only able to endure by keeping way too busy.

It did feel good to be here at the park though, with nothing to do but enjoy the feel of the warm sun in my face.

"We made this for ya Ei'... c'mon!" I heard Dot say. I looked dumbfounded at the newspaper kite she had laid on the table in front of me.

"That's right! I am telling you to go fly a kite!" she quipped. She stood there with her hands on her hips, tapping her foot.

I looked at the kite and then at my mom.

"Are you going to let her talk to you like that?" my mom giggled. "Go on! Have some fun dear."

I smiled, snapped up the kite and ran to join my other sisters at the water's edge.

"Go fly a kite, eh?" I sneered.

I slipped off my shoes and stood in the sand at the shore.

"I'll show you kids how to fly a kite."

I tossed the kite into the air and watched the stiff shore breeze carry it away while I slowly let some string out.

We laughed and watched our kites soar high in the air. I noticed an older couple sitting on a bench just up the shore and began to think about Jack and the first time I met him.

We had been writing to each other since he was in navigator's training in Texas. I was enjoying our letters, and we really seemed to hit it off right from the start, but we hadn't met in person yet.

One day in June, I was hanging some signs in the front windows of the lumberyard. I was looking out the windows at the beautiful day, when a bus stopped right in front of the store, blocking my view. When it pulled away, there was Jack, standing in the middle of the street, in his full dress uniform, holding a big green duffel bag.

He was home on leave and came straight there to surprise me. He told me he would take me anywhere I wanted to go that evening, likely expecting me to suggest dinner, a show, or a nightclub, but I chose here, along the riverside. We sat and talked for hours and watched the river flow by, just like that couple were doing today. Soon Jack will come home, and that will be us I thought to myself, letting more string out. The kite and my worries became smaller and smaller.

Time by the water was just what we all needed. Dad had been working long hours at the Packard plant since it had been converted over to building tanks for the war effort. Mom had taken a job at the five-and-dime to supplement the family income, and my sisters were doing most of the household chores while I worked just about non-stop. Food and gas were rationed to help the war effort. We all tended to the victory garden in the back yard and meat was a delicacy. But today, none of us had anything to do but relax and have fun. My sisters and I had a great time, we all had a delicious lunch, and the weather couldn't have been better. All too soon it was time to load everything back in the car and head back home.

As we drove home, I began to think of the first time Jack met my family. My dad is very protective of all of us, and he wasn't exactly thrilled when he realized the young serviceman I had been writing to was Jack Glide Sr.'s son. Dad believes hard work and responsibility are what makes a man. He only knew of Jack's dad and his reputation as a free living, fun loving, take-things-as-they-come-along kinda guy.

He was quietly stewing about it on the front porch of our two-story brick home on Cedargrove that day while the rest of us were inside, preparing for Jack's visit. He noticed a bright yellow Ford coupe roaring up the street, its bright blue fenders flapping in the wind as it rattled along.

"Hmphh… is the circus in town?" he grunted, and watched the car draw closer.

The car slowed and dissolved into a cloud of blue smoke as it pulled up and parked right in front of our house. It backfired loudly when the driver shut it off. The sound brought all of the neighbors to their windows.

His jaw clenched tightly on his cigar, and when the smoke cleared, he saw a polished young airman, who looked remarkably like a younger version of Jack Glide Sr. get out of it.

When my sisters, my mom and I ran out on the porch, Jack was coming up the sidewalk, looking like a mailman approaching a house full of bulldogs.

"Mom, Dad, everybody, this is Jack, the man I've been writing to," I said, standing at the top of the porch steps.

"Oh my word," Mom said, smiling coyly. She put her hand on her chin and my dad looked over at her and rolled his eyes.

"Wow," I heard Doe say from the back of the crowd.

"We've met. As did all the neighbors," Dad said, pointing his cigar up and down the street to those still gathered at their windows.

It was tense for a while, but Dad eventually learned to love Jack just as much as the rest of us. Perhaps it was how he saw Jack treating me, and the fact he seemed to be a responsible young man.

"What the devil," my dad said, startling me back to the present day.

As we drove down our street, I noticed Jack's dilapidated old car sitting in front of our house. We slowly coasted by and I noticed

Jack's dad sitting on the porch steps with his head down. He seemed to be reading something on a yellow piece of paper he held in his hands.

"Hey! Mr. Glide is here!" I said cheerfully.

Dad pulled up next to the curb and I jumped out. When I walked toward him, he looked up at me and I saw the look of sorrow in his face. I felt a chill go through me when he stood up and met us on the sidewalk.

"What's wrong?" I asked, reaching out to him.

I went numb when he stood there silent. I watched a small tear form on his cheek behind his thick glasses.

"It's Jack," he was finally able to choke out, "His plane has gone down."

He handed the telegram to my dad.

Is he… " I said, unable to voice my worst fear.

My dad put his glasses on, cleared his throat, and began to read the telegram out loud.

"The Secretary of War desires me to express his deep regret…"

"No," I gasped.

" …that your son, Sergeant Jack K. Glide, has been reported missing in action since Thirty September over Germany."

I put my arms around Mr. Glide and began to cry.

"Is he okay?" Rosie asked.

Dad continued to read the telegram.

"If further details or other information are received you will be promptly notified. Signed J.A. Ulio. The Adjutant General."

Dad finished and folded the telegram back up.

"Nobody knows much for right now," he added.

"What do you mean they don't know? Can't they find out?" Dot asked.

"I'm sure they will… in time."

"What do we do till then?" she asked.

"We wait and pray. There isn't anything else we can do."

I let go of Jack's dad, sat on the bottom step, and began to wipe my eyes.

"He's okay... I just know it," I said quietly.

"There, there, dear," my mom said, sitting next to me and putting her arm around me.

"No, mom. Remember that dream I had?" I explained. "I've seen him, and he's hurt, but he's going to be okay."

CHAPTER EIGHT

A Friendly Face

October 3, 1944
Tychow, Poland

I opened my eyes and focused on an older gentleman standing above me in a long, white lab coat. He had silvery, gray hair around the sides of his head and a shiny bald spot in the middle. A sad smile came over his face as he looked into my eyes.

"Hello. How are you feeling?" he asked in a perfect Midwestern American accent.

"Where am I? And who are you?" I asked as I sat up on an examination table and looked around the room.

The walls were light green and the floor was covered with small, clean, sea foam green tiles. My pants and flight jacket were draped over a nearby chair, and I was in my shirt and underwear. The old woman's dirty and blood-soaked scarf lay on a stainless steel table next to me, along with some surgical instruments. A clean bandage was wrapped around my upper thigh, covering my gunshot wound.

"My name is Dr. McKee. You are at Stalag Luft Number Four in occupied Poland," he said.

He walked around the side of the table and began to examine the knot in the back of my head.

"What's with the perfect English, Doc? Where ya from?" I asked.

"I am a doctor with the Red Cross. I'm from Lincoln, Nebraska."

"No kiddin'? I was in basic in Jefferson, Missouri." I said.

"What is your name? Where are you from?" he asked.

"My name is Jack Glide. I'm from Detroit," I answered.

"That's a pretty nasty gash on your head. Do you remember anything?"

"That's kinda the trouble, Doc. I remember too damn much but still haven't got any answers. My plane busted into pieces, I got shot on the way down by some locals, then an S.S. officer made me walk ten miles with this wound," I said, touching the bandages and wincing in pain.

The wound was still pretty tender, but the stinging and burning were subsiding.

"Then there was a long ride in a cattle train, which brought me here. The last thing I remember was tryin' to avoid bein' eaten alive by dogs and being stabbed in the ass with a bayonet. I tell ya Doc, I've had better days."

"Ah, yes. Captain Pickhardt and his welcome committee," he sighed and shook his head.

The name startled me. Pickhardt wasn't a place or thing after all. It was a person. I thought of the S.S. officer I'd seen running beside me.

"This Pickhardt fella… he got short black hair and act mad as a hatter?" I asked.

The Doc handed me my pants and I began to slip them back on. He looked around the room nervously before speaking.

"Yes. It is his idea to make all prisoners who arrive here make the same run through the dogs and bayonets as you did," he said quietly, casting a wary eye around the room before continuing.

"Pickhardt is one of three you need to watch out for here. They are all high ranking S.S., and they could care less if you live or die. In fact, they feel it's better if you die, and as slowly and painfully as possible. There are violations of the Geneva Convention being investigated, but... " He stopped short as two doctors speaking German entered the room.

"I removed some bullet fragments from your leg, and stitched up some wounds in your behind," he said in a professional manner, loud enough for the others to hear as they walked past, staring at me.

"Do you remember where you got the bump on your head?"

"Beats me Doc. I had it when I hit the ground," I replied as the two continued on their way and left the room.

"Hey! Where's my lighter and cigarettes?" I asked, fumbling through my pockets.

"Whatever the prisoners come through here with, they take. Watches, rings, memorabilia from home, cigarettes, it doesn't matter. It becomes theirs," he said.

He looked around the room again and reached inside his lab coat and took out my picture of Eileen. "I did manage to save this for you," he whispered, handing me the picture and picking up my flight jacket.

"Someone special, I assume?"

I watched him pick up a scalpel and make a small incision in the inner liner of my jacket just below the inside pocket.

"You better believe it Doc. And hey, thanks for keepin' that for me."

"We all have someone special we want to get back to. What's her name?" he asked as he took the picture and gently slid it inside the liner of my jacket.

He neatly stitched the seam so it was barely visible.

"Eileen, Eileen Shea. She's from Detroit too. Do me a favor Doc?"

"If possible, yes."

"If I give ya her address, could ya send her a note? Just to let her know I'm alive and okay."

"Sure. Just jot it down on this," He said, taking a small pad of paper and pencil out of the pocket of his lab coat.

"Thanks. This means a lot to me, Doc," I said as I scrawled down Eileen's address.

"Any other family you would like me to notify? Mom and Dad perhaps?" He asked.

"Nah. It's just Dad back home. Mom died when I was a kid. There's also my Aunt Margaret, but Eileen will let them know. Dad lives above the lumberyard where she works," I said.

Doc smiled and stuck the notepad back in his pocket.

"So, you are an airman I see… Eighth Air Force… impressive," he added, looking at the patches on the sleeve of my jacket before handing it back to me.

"Yep. I am… or I was… a radio operator on a B-17," I said, slipping my jacket back on.

"Sounds exciting… and dangerous. Where were you based?"

"Little town in England. Debach. Ever heard of it?"

"Oh, I probably have. There are so many that come through here."

I could hear the sound of heavy boots in the hallway getting closer.

"Do be careful, my friend, and remember who to watch out for," he said quietly, moments before the oldest and most decorated S.S. officer entered the room.

"Good afternoon, Colonel Bombach," Doc said.

The Colonel didn't say a word. He stopped and glared at me, twitching his riding crop behind his back.

"Are you quite finished with this one?" he asked the Doc in broken English, looking me up and down.

"Yes sir," Dr. McKee answered.

"Good. See that he meets with Captain Pickhardt immediately," he said.

He gave me an evil smile before turning and leaving the room.

"They all as nice as him?" I asked as the sounds of his boots on the tile floor faded in the distance.

"Unfortunately, yes," he sighed. "Don't tell anyone what I have told you, or we will both be in grave danger. Do you understand?"

"Don't worry Doc. Not one word from me," I said. "Glad to finally see a friendly face. Haven't seen too many since I hit the ground."

"No. I suppose not," the doctor chuckled.

I could hear the sound of heavy boots returning in the hallway at a faster pace. In the commotion just outside the room, I could hear the unmistakeable voice of Pickhardt.

"Was tut dieses Schwein noch hier? Warum vergueden Sie Bedarf an ihn?" Pickhardt shouted, bursting into the room with another German soldier.

"I was just finishing… " Doc explained.

Pickhardt shoved him aside.

"Machen sie SPAB!" he yelled at the doctor.

"Bekommen sie bewegendes, schwein!" he yelled at me, grabbing me by the arm and shoving me out the door.

As Pickhardt shoved me down the long hallway, I wondered what would happen next. I assumed it was time for my interrogation and it looked like it would be at the hands of the most dangerous man I had ever met.

As visions of outrunning the dogs and dodging the bayonets filtered through my mind, I remembered a time when I was a young boy and had a run-in with a dog and a group of thugs. It was during the Depression and I had found a Vernor's Ginger Ale bottle laying in the gutter along the street. It was like finding gold, and worth a whole nickel if returned to the store for deposit.

As I walked along the sidewalk thinking of all the candy I could put in my growling stomach, I forgot all about the O'Malley's huge German Shepard that would run up to the fence, just inches from me, and bark ferociously at me every time I passed by. Like clockwork, the dog met me at the fence and scared the hell out of me. Before I knew what I was doing, I bashed the dog in the head with the bottle, shattering it into pieces. The dog never bothered me after that, but the O'Malley brothers, all three of them twice my size, cleaned my clock the next day in a deserted alley. I acted as if their punches didn't hurt a bit. I was a wise ass, and laughed at them until they grew bored and left me alone.

I had no bottle to break over the heads of the dogs that haunted me now, and I had my doubts whether being a wise ass and laughing them off would tire Pickhardt and his goons into leaving me alone like it did with the O'Malleys. He seemed to like his job way too much. But, it was all I had. At least my family would soon know I was alive, thanks to the good doctor from Nebraska.

CHAPTER NINE

Welcome Wagon, They Ain't

October 3 1944
Tychow, Poland

Pickhardt and his goon took me to a small, dark, and dingy room. They sat me in a hard wooden chair and handcuffed my hands behind me and to the back of the chair, then left me. Time passed. I wasn't sure for how long, but it must have been at least a couple of hours. Maybe more. My whole body ached from sitting in the same position for so long. The room had a musty, sweaty smell that was beginning to make me feel sick to my stomach.

I wondered what would happen next. Captured officers such as pilots, co-pilots, navigators, and bombardiers were usually leaned on the hardest because of their knowledge of missions and targets, but a radio operator was a valuable prisoner too. I knew everything the officers did, and I also knew what radio frequencies that were used during missions. Should the Germans learn them, they could listen in and prepare for future attacks, maybe even ambush them. I had to keep that information to myself, no matter what. I had decided to tell Pickhardt I was a gunner. What he didn't know couldn't hurt me.

Suddenly, the door burst open and in walked Pickhardt with his riding crop and a manila folder tucked under his arm. He had that same angry look on his face. With him was a different fellow I hadn't seen before. He was as big as a mountain and wearing green army pants and a dingy, white sleeveless t-shirt with sweat stains down both sides. His head was shaved bald, he had huge muscular arms, shoulders and neck that made it look like his head was mounted directly to his body. He also had the same angry stare as Pickhardt.

"Hey Sunshine!" I said to Pickhardt. "Was beginnin' to wonder if you were ever comin' back. Who's no-neck there? Your wife?"

No-neck responded by punching me square in the gut, knocking every bit of air out of my lungs. Damn, that hurt. I gathered my strength and gasped for air, wondering if being a wise ass was gonna work after all.

"Nice to meet you too," I wheezed out.

Pickhardt's expression never changed. He took the manila folder out from under his arm and pulled out two photos.

"I thought you might vant to zee some of your cowardly vuurk firsthand," he said, holding the photos in front of me.

One of them was of a young, dark-haired woman lying dead in the street in a pool of her own blood. There was a hole in the middle of her forehead and I could see a portion of her skull behind her ear was missing. Her brains were oozing out of the hole. Her eyes were wide open and her mouth was open slightly. Blood ran from between her painted lips. She bore a chilling resemblance to Eileen. The other was picture was of a small child lying dead and horribly mutilated. His little body was riddled with bullet holes and he was also lying in a pool of his own blood.

"Nah, ya got the wrong guy, Sunshine. I'm an airman three miles up. I drop bombs on military targets. These people were killed with small arms, at close range… maybe with that Walther," I said, nodding toward his pistol.

No-neck swatted with the back of his hand right on the knot on the back of my head, sending me and the chair to the floor. I was seeing stars, and my head hurt like hell as he picked both me and the chair up and slammed us down, upright and against the wall.

"Thanks, Gertrude. I had an itch there an' ya got it for me," I sneered.

Pickhardt began to pace the room, stopping in front of me to poke at my gunshot wound with the pointed end of his riding crop.

"Vee need some information from you," he said.

"I ain't givin' ya nuthin' more than name, rank, and serial number," I said, cutting him off before he could finish.

"You obviously don't know vhere you are," he said, pushing harder on the riding crop. "Or vhat could happen to you. Why, you could have easily bled to death when you vere shot," he said.

I felt some stitches popping from the pressure he was putting on them.

"Sometimes missing airmen never show up, sometimes ve find zhem in terrible shape," he said.

"Shot? That was just a flesh wound an' I'm pretty tough," I said, trying hard to conceal the pain he was causing.

"And it was the other leg… in case you're interested," I lied.

He went back to pacing and tapping the riding crop on his hand.

"I von't be bored with your name, rank, and zerial number Sergeant Glite. I already know all zat… and much more," he hummed.

"So tell me, vhat was your position up zhere?" he asked, pointing toward an imaginary sky.

"I was a gunner," I replied, which was met by a punch in the jaw from no-neck.

"Liar!" Pickhardt shouted. "Vould you like to know vhat I know about you?"

I sat motionless, saying not a word as he continued to pace back and forth.

"Shall ve start by saying you vere a radio operator on a B-17, not a gunner?" he asked, looking at something on the manila folder while pacing.

"You vere born in Detroit, Mee-sha-gin. Your mother died

when you vere eight years zold, correct? Zee only family you have left is your father and your dear Aunt Mary," he continued on.

"Let's not forget your fiancée, Eileen. Eileen Shea is it not, ya? And vhat vas her address? 14514 Cedargrove, Detroit, Mee-sha-gin, ya?" he said as he stopped and looked directly into my eyes, giving me a wicked smile.

"Beautiful girl, no doubt. It vould be a shame to zee zomzing like zhis happen to her," he said, holding the photo of the dead woman in front of me again.

"Vee auf spies een your country too. It vould be very easy to find her. So… you can tell us vhat ve'd like to know, or maybe ve can do to your fiancée vhat you cowards do to our vimmen and children, ya?"

"You touch one hair on her head an' I'll kill you!" I growled.

I saw no-necks fist coming at me a split second before it met my right eye, knocking me and the chair over again. He picked the chair back up and slammed me down in front of Pickhardt.

"It is NOT your choice who liff's, and who dies, it ezz mine," Pickhardt hissed. "I dezide eef, vhere, vhen, und even how zlowly either of you die, understood? Now, if you cooperate and give us your radio frequencies zee two auf you vill live a long, happy life together, ya? If you don't… " Pickhardt shrugged his shoulders, "you may never see her again."

I sat motionless and said nothing. How the hell does he know so much about me? Other than getting my aunt's name wrong and being a year off on when mom died, he seemed to know everything about me. Where the hell did he get Eileen's address? The only people that knew that were me and my friend Mike from back in basic, maybe a few others back in Debach.

"Vell?" Pickhardt asked, tapping the riding crop on my leg. "Ve are vaiting."

"Okay. I'll tell ya what I know," I said under my breath.

"Excellent!" Pickhardt said, smiling for the first time. "So, tell me vhat I need to know," he said, leaning closer to me.

"I know you NEED to go to Goddamn hell!" I yelled, and spit in his face.

Out of the corner of my good eye, I saw no-neck clench his fists together and swing them at my head like he was swinging a baseball bat. I heard the thud his fists made when they made contact with my head, just before the lights went out.

CHAPTER TEN

A Damn Lonely Place

October 5, 1944
Stalag Luft Four
Tychow, Poland

I looked out the window of the airplane at the calm, clear blue sky. The song "Sentimental Journey" was softly playing in the background as we silently floated along.

"Bombardier, do you have a visual of our target?" I heard LaFlame ask.

"Affirmitive Captain, she's coming into view," O'Neil responded.

"Bomb bay doors open," LaFlame said.

As the doors opened, I could smell an overwhelming stench of rotten cabbage. I leaned forward and looked out the open doors. Where the hell was that smell coming from?

"She's all yours, O'Neil. Line us up and drop our eggs so we can go home," LaFlame said.

I wished he would drop them soon so we could close the doors and get rid of that awful goddamn smell.

"Bombs away!" I heard O'Neil yell.

I watched the bombs fall from the plane. They just kept falling and falling. It seemed like there were hundreds of them. Where the hell were they all coming from?

"Let's get the hell outta here!" Malloy shouted as soon as the last bomb cleared.

Suddenly, a huge explosion rocked and rattled the whole plane.

"What the hell was that?" I yelled. I looked at Malloy who was staring back at me with wide eyes.

The sky outside grew darker and darker. I could hear an ominous growling sound drawing closer and louder. Something was out there, heading right for us.

In slow motion, a propeller blade slashed a hole in the side of plane, right in front of where Malloy was standing. With slow, methodical chops, it continued to slash away at the fuselage, seeming to gain strength with each one. Malloy was swatting at it, trying to fight it off and push it back out of the plane. I tried to get up and help him, but I couldn't move. A wave of intense heat washed through the plane as the prop kept tearing away at the plane, leaving Malloy with less room to stand with each bite. The music was playing louder and the cabbage smell was getting stronger. In a ball of flames, the engine that the killer prop was attached to burst through the side of the plane, scooping up Malloy in its cowling just as the prop finished chopping off the back of the plane.

"Nooooo!" I yelled as I watched the engine carry away Malloy, who was helplessly reaching out to me.

I was screaming as loud as I could, but no sound was coming from me. The plane turned sharply upward, sending me into the ceiling, then quickly started to nosedive, knocking me down on the floor. The engines were screaming, the music was deafening, and the plane was falling fast. I could see my parachute hanging from a hook on the wall near the radio and tried to reach for it. The more I stretched out, the farther away it seemed. I just couldn't get closer. When did I hang it there? I could have sworn I had it on.

A stream of white fog seemed to roll in from the hole in the rear of the plane, circle around beside my parachute pack, and take on the appearance of a shadowy person hovering there. It seemed to reach up and shake my parachute from the wall, knocking it behind me. As quickly as the chute fell, the ghostly figure darted behind me as well. Did I see wings?

It felt as if something or someone was picking me up as I began to slowly move toward the dark sky outside the plane. I tried to grab behind me for my parachute and realized I had it on.

I turned back toward the opening I was being drawn to and gasped. The ghostly figure was now floating directly in front of me. It was a woman, and I could see right through her. She hovered gently, flapping a pair of beautiful silvery, white wings, and held her arms out toward me. She drifted backward, toward the opening. It felt as if she were pulling me out of the wreckage, yet she wasn't touching me. She looked right into my eyes and gave me a smile. It was a smile I instantly recognized.

"Mom?" I heard myself shout as I leapt up. The figure was gone. So was the noise of the engines, the tattered plane, the falling sensations, the loud music, everything was gone. Everything except for that stench of rotten cabbage, and that was stronger than ever.

I found myself sitting up on a straw filled mattress on a small bed, in a cold sweat, panting heavily. The room I was in was very tiny with barely enough room for the bed I was sitting on. A stainless steel commode was in one corner, and a little wooden table was in the other. At one end of the room was a heavy steel door with no doorknob. At the other was a window that had been painted over from the outside. Heavy iron bars hung on the inside. The room was dimly lit by streams of light that pierced through spots in the window where paint had flaked off or worn thin.

The more alert I became, the more I remembered. I was beginning to feel the beating no-neck had given me. I felt like I'd been run over by a truck, my mouth was bone dry, and hunger pangs were gnawing at my insides.

I leaned against the wall beside the bed, pulled my legs up in front of me, put my head in my hands, and began to think about the nightmare I just had. I'd been having variations of it every time I closed my eyes, and each time it just seemed to get more bizarre. This was the first time I had seen who the ghostly figure was, or who I thought it was. Could it have really been her that took me out of the plane? Or was it just another odd thing that popped into the dream? Maybe it was my hunger, thirst, or the knot on the back of my head playing tricks on me.

"Mom, if it was you watchin' over me, keep it up," I said, staring at the walls.

I remember the day she died as if it were yesterday. I was rushing home from school, hoping she would be feeling good that day. She had been sick for quite a while, but my stories of how my day went always seemed to make her feel better. If she was feeling well enough, we might be able to finish the story she had been reading to me about a remote chain of islands in the Pacific Ocean. I couldn't remember the name of them back then, but I enjoyed curling up on her lap and looking at the pictures while she told me the story about them until it was time to start making supper before dad came home.

I thought of how ironic it was that the name of that island chain was the Hawaiian Islands.

As I neared our house, I saw dad sitting on the steps outside our front door. Why was he home so early? And why did he look so sad?

He told me to sit down beside him on the steps and put his arm around me. He tried to come up with words my young mind could understand for what had just happened. Eventually, he simply told me that mom had gone to heaven.

"But, she never finished our story," I said.

How could she go without me? When was she coming back?

Why did she have to leave me? I didn't like any of dad's answers to the many questions I had. It just wasn't fair.

My life was never the same after that. I became a handful for dad, and more and more, he found comfort in the bottle he kept hidden in his dresser drawer. It wasn't long after mom died when the Depression hit and dad lost his job. I was sent to live with my Aunt Margaret and Uncle John, while dad struggled to find work.

The cabbage stench was starting to overwhelm me, and the more I followed my nose, it seemed to be coming from a bowl on the table across the room. I moved over to the edge of the bed and picked the bowl up. In a stream of light coming in the window, I could see it was full of cooked cabbage that was beginning to turn black on the edges. It was floating in a dank, brownish liquid. The smell made my stomach turn, but I remembered eating a lot of things I didn't like during the Depression, before I went to live with my aunt. Amazing what you'll eat if you're hungry enough.

I tried to bring the bowl to my mouth to get a drink of the liquid, but gagged at the smell. I tried to hold my breath and take a quick drink, but that didn't work either. I'd eaten and drank some awful things in my life, but this was the worst.

"You expect me to eat this shit?" I asked no one, putting the bowl back down.

I let out a long, lonely sigh and leaned back against the wall. Visions of Malloy being torn from the plane played through my mind again. Did all the others meet a similar horrible fate? How many were still in the plane when it slammed into the ground? Were Ortlip and I the only ones spared? If whatever hit the plane had been eight feet farther forward, I wouldn't be here.

I wondered how long I had been here and how long it would be until Pickhardt would come back for me. At least I was able to give the doctor Eileen's address before Pickhardt worked me over, so she would know I was alive. I hoped I would be able to write home soon myself.

I froze as I suddenly realized how Pickhardt knew so much about me. I had told the doctor all my family information, including Eileen's address. I had told him what happened to me since the crash. I told him I was a radio operator. That explains why it took so long for Pickhardt to get around to questioning me. He must have been grilling the good doctor. I could only imagine what they had done to the poor old man. I wondered if he even got the chance to send a note.

I sat up on the edge of the bed and looked at the cabbage again. Maybe if I picked the cabbage out and took the rotten edges off, I could get it past my nose quick enough to get it down. I couldn't help but think of the time my Aunt Margaret sent me to a small farm across the street for some eggplant. The farm had a field of eggplant as far as I could see, but I wasn't looking forward to eating it. I hated the damn stuff. I came home an hour later, empty-handed, and told her they were all out of it. After gettin' my ass tanned, I was sent back. Looking at the cabbage, I wished for a plate of Aunt Margaret's eggplant instead, but this was what I had.

I grabbed a handful of cabbage and felt a stabbing pain in my fingertips.

"Ouch! Dammit!" I said, recoiling my hand. I held it up to the light and saw blood dripping from my fingertips.

"What the hell?" I said.

I picked up the bowl with the palms of my hands and held it up to the light coming through the window. Mixed with the cabbage, I could see hundreds of small shards of broken glass.

"You SONOFABITCH!" I screamed.

I stood up and threw the bowl at the door, shattering it and strewing cabbage and glass all over the floor. I clutched my hand into a fist to stop the bleeding and began to pace the room, muttering to myself. I kicked the table, sending it into the wall and eventually upside down onto the bed. I went to the door and kicked it, but it didn't budge. I kept kicking it repeatedly until I settled back down on the end of the bed and fumed about what they tried to do to me. How dare that son of a bitch!

I bent down and picked up a good sized triangular piece of the bowl up off of the floor. I slid the table across the bed and sat it on my lap. On the bottom of the table, I scratched a mark in the wood, marking the first day, and sat the table back up in the corner. Then I hid the piece of broken bowl in my jacket pocket.

"C'mon back now, you goddamn sonofabitch," I muttered to myself, staring at the door.

CHAPTER ELEVEN

My Birthday Wish

October 15, 1944
Detroit, Michigan

Nineteen candles flickered gently on top of the chocolate cake with white icing that sat before me on our dining room table. The sound of my family singing "Happy Birthday" faded into the background as my mind drifted off.

I thought of how Jack always started his letters to me: "How's my Honey? You still love me? Sure you're not lyin'??" It always put a smile on my face, no matter how I felt. It made me feel like he was right there with me. One letter he sent startled me. It began with I'm okay—I've been in a crash but I am fine.

Jack had signed up for glider pilot training and his first (and last) attempt at landing didn't end well. He sent a small fragment of the plane with the note saying not to worry—he was tough and had been through a lot worse than that. He survived that crash. I wished with all my heart he'd made it through this one.

"Time to make a wish, dear," I heard my mom say.

"We all know what you're wishin', Dollface. We're all wishin' the same," my dad said, "let's all blow together to make sure it comes true."

We all gathered close together and gave a mighty blow. The candles all went out quickly and we sat in awkward silence, watching the small wisps of smoke trail off of the candles. It hadn't really been that long since we received the telegram notifying us that his plane had gone down, but it felt like years. Hearing he was alive and okay really would be the best birthday present I could hope for.

My heart skipped a beat with the sound of the doorbell.

"I'll get it!" I shouted, leaping up and running to the door. I flung the door open to see Jack's dad standing there.

"Look at you! Prettier than ever! Happy birthday, Red…" he said, giving me a hug. "This is for you."

He handing me a colorful birthday card, and an envelope with a return address from Jack's base in England.

"Did they find him?!" I gasped, anxious for news, but worried at the same time.

"No. Not yet… but they're hopin' to. This is a letter from his chaplain. I thought you would like to have it," he said.

"Oh, thank you!" I said.

"Whatsit say?" my sisters asked in unison.

"Let's see… " I said, opening the letter.

My family gathered around me. I cleared my throat and began to read it aloud—

Dear Mr. Glide;

The War Department has already informed you that your son, Sergeant Jack K. Glide, is missing in action.

The Commanding General of the 8th Air Force, as well as our Group Commander, Lt. Col. Elbert Helton, have asked me to convey to you a word of encouragement at this particular time. The phrase "missing in action" is so often misinterpreted by the folks back home, that we think it wise to allay any undue apprehension that may be yours. The percentage of men who are now classified as "missing in action," but who are eventually heard from, is usually high.

We, the members of this Bombardment Group, are in hope of hearing some good news for your son's safety. You should be of the same firm confidence that someday he shall return to you again.

I think it only fair to warn you that impatience for some definite news will be your greatest trial. Weeks' perhaps months, may come and go and still no word to buoy up your hopes. In such cases of which we speak, communications work slowly, and a certain routine must, of necessity, be carried out. Do not let the time element undermine your perseverance.

Before each of our combat missions, the opportunity of receiving the Sacrament of Penance and Holy Communion is afforded to our men of Catholic faith. I know as a priest that you will be thankful to hear that your son was faithful to his obligation in this regard.

Sgt. Glide has always been a credit to the U.S. Army Air Force. His attention to duty is worthy of your imitation. For now, it is your duty to trust that Almighty God will watch over him in this time of separation. We are confident you shall not fail.

If you receive any word that Sgt. Glide is a prisoner of war, I would appreciate your sending this information as soon as possible.

Sincerely,

James T. McCarthy, Captain, Group Chaplain

The room went silent, except for the sound of me folding the letter and stuffing it back in the envelope.

"Well, he did say the percentage of men found is high, dear." my mom said. "We'll just do as he says and keep praying. Won't you come in Mr. Glide?" she added.

"Oh dear! Silly me, standing here in the doorway!" I said. "Please, do come in."

"Your mom is right, Red." Mr. Glide said as he came in and took off his hat and coat. My sister Dot took them and hung them on the coat rack behind the door.

"Lookie here, Red… if there's one thing I know, it's that that damn boy can go through anything and make it," he said as he put his arm around me while we walked to the dining room.

"We were just going to have cake and ice cream… you're just in time!" my mom said. "Please… sit down and make yourself comfortable."

"Thanks," he said, pulling out my chair, then sitting down next to me.

"Have I ever told you about little junior and old lady Lipskey's cats?" he asked.

"No, I don't believe so," I answered.

My mind was a million miles away, still taking in all the letter said. It did suggest there was a good chance of hearing something good, but also hinted it could be a long time.

"Damnedest thing I ever saw!" Mr. Glide bellowed. "He hated them cats, and old lady Lipskey musta had pert near a hunnert of 'em. Anyway, I look out the kitchen window an' I see little Jack tyin' two of 'em's tails together. What's that boy up to now, I said to myself." My family listened intently to his story.

"Just then, I seen him pick them cats up and toss 'em over old lady Lipskey's clothesline."

My dad chuckled and the look on his face suggested he could see Jack doing that.

"Them damn cats were screamin' and clawin' at each other,

67

tryin' to get down. Fur was flyin' and ya could hear the commotion up and down the whole block. I ran outside, gettin' there just in time to see old lady Lipskey takin' her broom to his backside."

My mom and dad were both chuckling under their breath. A smile came across my face. Jack did have a mischievous side. I thought it to be one of his better traits.

"What happened to the cats?" my sister Rosie asked.

"Awww, they was alright Rosie. Jack wound up gettin' the worst of it. Old lady Lipskey told him he got 'em up there, he was gettin' em down. He looked at me like I was gonna help him out, but I told him, You heard her! Get to it boy!"

"How did he get them down?" Doe asked.

"It wudn't easy," Mr. Glide said. "He tried pullin' em apart, but they'd dig their claws in him. He did manage to get a hold of one of 'em and try to lift it over the clothesline, but as he lifted it, the other one was comin' down, and dug his claws into his backside. He let go of the other cat, which made the one on his backside let go… trouble was, now he had the first cat comin' down in his face."

My sisters were laughing out loud. I began to laugh as well, seeing this play out in my mind.

"Old lady Lipskey eventually got her scissors and held one cat and cut the string while he held the other one," Mr Glide said.

My mom set plates of cake and ice cream in front of us. We all started eating and continued to giggle about the story.

"I guess my point is… " Mr. Glide said between bites, "he's been goin' through stuff like that all his life. Iff'n it wasn't cats or dogs, it was just plain hard times. The Depression… losin' his mom… stuff like that toughens ya up, ya know. If there's any chance… " his voice trailed off.

"I know," I said. "The waiting is hard, but I'm still sure he is okay."

"Here's to good news… and may it come soon!" my dad said, raising his glass of water up as a toast.

"Amen to that!" my mom said as we clinked our glasses together.

"I was thinking about his other crash earlier. He did survive that one," I said.

The room was silent except for the sound of silverware on plates. All I hoped for was some good news for my birthday, but here it was late afternoon, and still nothing.

We finished our cake and ice cream and talked for awhile, trying hard to stay on upbeat subjects. It was obvious we all had Jack, wherever he was, whatever was happening to him, and most importantly, if he was alive, in every thought.

After Mr. Glide left, I helped my mom and sisters clean up. When we were done, I grabbed my coat and hat.

"I'm going to church to light a candle," I sighed.

"Wait up! We'll go with you," my sisters said.

As the four of us walked down the sidewalk, I was already saying an extra prayer that news would come sooner than later. The good chaplain was right. Waiting is the greatest trial.

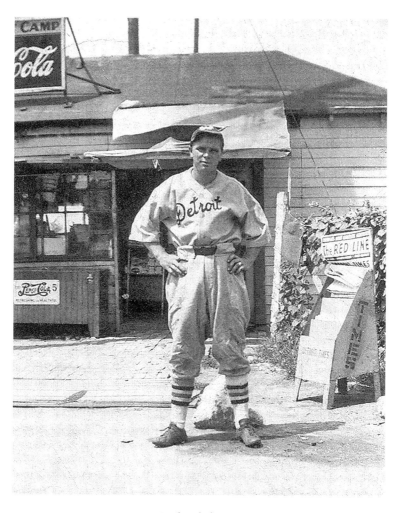

Jack Glide Jr.
Detroit Tigers bat boy

CHAPTER TWELVE

You Look Familiar

October 26, 1944
Stalag Luft Four
Tychow, Poland

The sun was shining brightly and a nice breeze was blowing in from right field. It was the perfect day for baseball here at Navin Field.

The White Sox were in town. I stood silently, dressed in my bat boy uniform at my position near the warm up circle along the third base line. The Sox catcher Moe Berg was warming up the pitcher, Tommy Thomas. The rest of the team was tossing balls out on the field.

"Can I have my bat, son?" I heard someone say. I looked up and saw my favorite Tiger player, Charlie Gehringer, towering in front of me.

"Sure, Mr. Gehringer," I said handing him the huge bat I had been holding.

"Got something on your mind, kid?" he asked.

"I'm just worried I guess. And I don't feel too good," I responded.

"Worryin' shortens your life, son," Gehringer said, "best to forget about your worries and move on. Probably make you feel better too."

This was odd. Gehringer is known to be a man of few words. He is nicknamed The Mechanical Man. Teammate and manager

Mickey Cochrane jokes that he says "Hello" on opening day; "Goodbye" on closing day, and hits .350 in between. Yet here he is, giving me advice.

"I dunno, Mr. Gehringer," I said, "I hurt all over. Especially my leg and my head. I feel feverish too. What's gonna happen to me?" I added, noticing I was a grown man, and wearing a tattered Army Air Corps flight suit.

"Awww... come here, my little man," a woman's voice said.

I looked up and saw my mom wearing Gehringer's uniform, reaching out to pick me up. I was a small child, wearing the white button down shirt and dark blue wool shorts I had when I was a kid. She picked me up and cuddled me in her arms.

"Mommy will make you feel a-a-all better... " she cooed.

"Sergeant Glide!" I heard someone shout. I instinctively stood at attention. My pilot, Lt. Col. LaFlame, was standing in front of me. We were both in our dress uniforms.

"You can't stand here and play ball all day! We have a mission to fly!" He barked.

"Yes sir!" I responded, snapping him a salute. All of the players had stopped practicing, and were standing on both sides of the infield. The Tigers stood in silence along the third base line, the White Sox along the first base line. Both teams watched us as LaFlame and I walked past them toward the Purple Heart which sat silently in the middle of center field.

At the end of the group of Tiger players, Charlie Gehringer stood leaning on his bat.

"Good luck, kid. And stop that damn worryin'!" he said, tipping his cap and giving me a smile.

"Play ball!" I heard an umpire shout as we cleared the infield and neared the plane. Before I climbed up into the escape hatch under the nose of the plane, I stopped and looked back at the players again. The Sox had taken their positions on the field and Tommy

Thomas was ready to throw the first pitch of the game. Charlie Gehringer stood at the plate swinging his bat back and forth, awaiting the pitch. It would likely be a fast ball, high and inside. Thomas loved brushing the batter back with the first pitch.

I waved to Gehringer before I climbed into the Purple Heart, but noticed something different about him. He had an evil grin on his face, and he didn't look the same. It wasn't Gehringer batting... it was Pickhardt.

I settled into my position in the plane just as the engines began to start up and watched the game from the window of the radio room. The first pitch was a fast ball that made Pickhardt leap back from the batter's box. What'd I tell ya?

"Ball one!" The ump shouted. Pickhardt stepped back in the batter's box, tapped the plate with the end of his bat, and readied for the next pitch. He had an angry look on his face and one eye on the Purple Heart as we took off and circled the field.

The next pitch was another fast ball, right down the middle. Pickhardt swung with all his might, hitting the ball directly at the Purple Heart. He stood there and laughed like a madman as the ball closed in on us. When the ball hit the side of the plane there was a huge explosion. Fire was everywhere. I heard crew members crying out in pain as the plane began to fall from the sky.

• • •

"Huhhh... " I heard myself utter, waking with a jolt, realizing I was still in solitary. I sat up on the side of the bed and tried to shake off the remaining cobwebs in my head. My bullet wound hurt like hell and my leg was swollen to the point that my pants were very tight around it. I was having trouble focusing on the dark confines of the cell. My whole body ached and I was sweating like a dog, but felt chilled to the bone. There was light coming through the small areas of chipped paint on the window.

I thought about the dream I just had and remembered the summer that I actually was a bat boy for the Detroit Tigers. I was eleven years old and a ticket taker caught me sneaking into Navin Field to watch a ballgame. I was scared stiff as I stood in the shadow of the man. He was big as a mountain, towering over me with his hands on his hips and an angry look on his face.

"Whatcha doin' here, boy?" he growled at me.

I didn't know what to say. I didn't have a ticket or the money for one, and I sure didn't want to get sent home to my dad for a whoopin' for sneaking into the stadium.

"I... I'm here to try out for bat boy," I lied.

Next thing I knew, I was standing in front of the Tigers Manager, Mickey Cochrane, sticking to my lame excuse.

He must have felt sorry for me, and I couldn't believe my ears when I heard him say "Get this kid a uniform."

The job didn't pay a dime, but I got to see every home game that year along with a hot dog and a box of Cracker Jacks. I felt like a king.

My stomach let out a long low rumbling growl. I wondered how long I'd been in here, and how long it had been since I had eaten anything. I honestly couldn't remember.

On the table, I saw a small loaf of black bread and a glass of dirty water. I reached out and picked up the loaf of bread and held it up to the window and looked at it closely in the light. It seemed okay, so I broke a chunk off and felt it for hidden objects before putting it in my mouth. I could taste a hint of sawdust in it as I devoured it. When I finished the loaf, I looked in the glass of water before sipping it down.

I picked up the small table, turning it over on my lap. Scratched in the bottom were four sets of lines all with a line scratched through them marking twenty days. I reached into my pocket and took out the shard of the bowl and scratched a shaky line, marking day twenty-one.

"How long are you gonna keep me in here?" I muttered at the walls. Sitting here alone in the dark for so long was beginning to wear on me. The silence was deafening. Even another beating seemed like a good thing, if it meant seeing or hearing anything again.

I heard the sound of footsteps approaching outside the door along with the sound of keys jingling together. I saw the shadows of a pair of feet under my door and the sound of the lock being opened.

My mind filled with excitement, anticipation, and fear. I was getting out of this hell, but what was in store for me now? Who was on the other side of the door?

The door flung open, sending a ray of light into my cell that was as bright as the sun. I shielded my eyes and looked towards the open door, making out the silhouette of a man standing there. He appeared to have a rifle in his hands.

"Stehen Sie auf! Jetzt!!" He shouted at me, reaching in and grabbing me by the arm. "Bekommen Sie das Bewegen!!" he screamed, shoving me out the door.

The brightness of the hallway outside my cell was almost too much for my eyes to take. I squinted and took in the commotion all around me. Guards were opening other solitary cells and dragging prisoners out and shoving us all down a long narrow hallway. I don't know where they were taking us, but they sure seemed to be in a hell of a hurry. When we reached the end of the hallway, they shoved me out a door. I noticed we were outside of the heavily fenced-in prison camp and on the same road we came into camp on. I was overwhelmed by the smell of fresh air and pine trees as the guards kept pushing us quickly up the road.

Ahead of us, a train sat idle on the tracks. I could make out Pickhardt and Bombach standing in front of a small red boxcar with the faded black lettering of *Italia National* on the side. The car was open, and there was a ramp leading into it. They were both talking to another officer of some sort.

As the guards led us past the officers, I recognized the third officer as none other than the friendly man I knew as Dr. McKee. He wasn't wearing his lab coat. Instead, he was wearing a German Gestapo officer's uniform. I slowed down and stared at him as I walked past him.

"You son of a bitch," I muttered, realizing I'd been had.

"Beweg Dich! Jetzt!" a soldier yelled at me, shoving me up the ramp.

The first thing I noticed as I began to enter the boxcar was that this one was remarkably clean, and had fresh straw on the floor. I looked at the prisoners already in the car, and recognized some of them from the ride here, but all of them looked beaten half to death. In a corner in the back of the car, I saw Willie Strong on the floor, curled up in a big ball. I went over and sat next to him. He was shaking like a leaf and mumbling.

They loaded thirty-seven of us on the train before the guards closed and locked the doors. All of us appeared to have gone through hell since the last time we were together. As the train lurched ahead and began to move down the tracks, I wondered where we were going now.

At least the conditions in this train were better than the last one. I thought about how I had been tricked by the Gestapo Officer posing as an American and how freely I gave him information. I wasn't sure where they were taking us now, but I was sure of one thing. I was keeping my damn mouth shut from now on.

CHAPTER THIRTEEN

The Long Ride

October 27, 1944
Somewhere East of Tychow

"Willie… " I said, nudging him, "you okay?" Willie jumped like I scared him half to death and muttered something I couldn't understand.

"Your friend looks like he's in pretty rough shape," a young army sergeant said, moving in closer, extending his hand out to me. "Leon Swisher," he said, shaking my hand. "This guy a member of your crew?"

"No," I said, "he was on the same train that brought me here. All I know about him is his name is Willie, and he's from Detroit, same as me," I replied.

I noticed Leon didn't appear to be as beaten as the rest of us. In fact, other than his uniform being dirty and a little tattered, he barely had a scratch on him.

"I've got some medical training, plus some good ole mountain remedies," Leon said. "Let's see if we can help this guy out."

I said nothing as he knelt in front of Willie and reached out to touch him.

"Willie… " he said, giving him a gentle shake.

"NOOOOO!!!" GET AWAY FROM ME!!" Willie screamed out, huddling in a ball and covering his head with his hands.

"Whoa there, my friend!" Leon shouted. "I'm an American! I'm tryin' to help. Just relax… "

77

Willie continued to huddle into a ball and was shaking like a leaf.

"Willie! It's me, Jack, the other guy from Detroit," I said. "We're on a train out of that hellhole… no one is gonna hurt you."

I continued, keeping a wary eye on Leon.

"This guy has some medical training and just wants to help." I said.

Willie began to calm down, eventually taking his hands from his face. The bruises on his face seemed much more severe than the rest of us. He opened his eyes and looked up at me. I could see the pure fear in them. What the hell did they do to this guy?

"I need you to relax, so I can check out your wounds," Leon told him. Willie remained huddled up on the floor, mumbling to himself.

"It's okay," I told him. "Let him take a look at you."

Willie began to stir and slowly roll over on his back. His face was covered with wounds of some sort, but they didn't appear to be bruises; it was more like deep burns and pieces of flesh were missing. I could see more wounds on his chest protruding from the opening in the top of his shirt. Leon unbuttoned his shirt and carefully opened it.

"Good God!" Leon exclaimed.

Looking at the sight made us both sick. A huge swastika was burned into Willie's chest.

"Those sick bastards took a branding iron to this man!" Leon said. "We have to keep these wounds clean, or he's gonna get infected!" he added, gently brushing dirt and cloth fibers from the swastika.

I carefully picked dirt and pieces of straw from the burn wounds in Willie''s face.

"Ya say you're both from Detroit?" Leon asked me as we tended to Willie.

"Yeah," I answered.

"I'm from Pennsylvania… little town of Waynesboro," he told me.

"My best friend is from Pittsburg," I said, thinking of Mike Postek. "My pilot was from Pennsylvania, too," I added, sadly remembering LaFlame and the last few minutes aboard the Purple Heart.

"What are their names?" He asked. "While were at it, where were you based? What brought you here… all that. May as well get to know each other."

A vision of Dr. McKee smiling at me popped into my mind.

"Ya know what, it doesn't matter," I told him. "If you don't mind, I'll just concentrate on takin' care of my friend here."

"Suit yourself," Leon said. "Although I don't know what's suddenly got your mouth slammed tighter than a gnat's asshole stretched over a fencepost."

"Just not in a talkative mood these days," I said, wincing in pain as I shifted my weight off of my leg.

"That looks pretty swollen," Leon said. "What happened there?"

I sat in silence pondering my answer.

"Gunshot wound," I answered.

"Lemme take a look at it," Leon said.

I thought about whether I should or not. I'm still wasn't sure about this guy… then again, my leg does hurt like hell.

"C'mon dammit! Drop 'em and let me look at your wound!" Leon shouted.

Reluctantly, I unbuttoned my pants and lowered them past my knees. I noticed my leg was swollen nearly half again the size of my other leg as I watched Leon carefully pull back the bandages. A rotten stench filled my nose as he finished removing them. Dark blood and a slimy green puss was oozing from the wound.

"You got one hell of an infection, my friend," Leon said, studying the wound. "It's gonna hurt like hell, but I've got to clean this out. Otherwise your gonna lose this leg!"

I nodded in agreement.

Leon pulled a small pocket knife from his pants pocket and began to carefully cut away at the infection. I screamed out in pain, but knew it was something that had to be done.

"So tell me, Leon… " I said, catching my breath, "How is it we're all beat to hell and have had everything taken from us, yet you're barely scratched and still have that pocket knife?"

"Kind of a long story… " Leon chuckled.

"You're the one who said we got nothin' but time," I answered.

"I take it you didn't see me when they were shoving you down that hallway," Leon said.

I thought about the commotion and how the light was hurting my eyes.

"Nope. Can't say I did," I told him.

"I was in a group of prisoners that had just arrived," he said. "We were in the hallway when they led all of you guys out. Willie here was the first one they dragged past us," he added, digging deeper into my leg with his knife.

"And you made it through that madman Pickhardt's dogs unharmed?" I asked, wincing in pain.

"What dogs?" Leon asked.

"The ones that greet ya when ya get off the train," I responded.

"I didn't see any dogs," Leon said. "just a mess of Red Cross inspectors. And the same three Jerries that were there when we got on the train"

I started to grow more suspicious with his story.

"So how did you wind up on this train?" I asked.

"Actually, it's BACK on this train. And I took two steps forward."

"What the hell is that supposed to mean?" I asked.

"When they were shovin' you guys down the hallway I seen they were taking you through the same door to the outside I had just come through," Leon began to explain. "They weren't payin' a whole lot of attention to us, so when there was a crowd of ya in front of me, I lowered my head, took two steps forward and blended in. Next thing I knew, I was being shoved out the door. I didn't know where they were takin' you, but I figgered if I got outside again, I could escape. Here, hold this," he said, handing me his pocket knife and taking a small flask out of the inside of his coat. "Besides, I seen what they had done to all of you, and it HAD to be safer outside with all those inspectors around," he said, pouring alcohol into my wound.

I grit my teeth as my wound burned like the fires of hell.

"When we got outside, the inspectors were gone. It was just those three Jerry S.S. goons and all those guards. I had no choice but to get back on this train—the same one that brought me in." Leon said.

The story seemed pretty far-fetched to me. How the hell does someone just walk out of a prison camp unnoticed?

Leon poured alcohol on my bandage and flipped it over, tying it to my leg, clean side down.

"This is the best I can do for ya, my friend," he said. "Dunno where this train is goin', but I hope it gets us there fast. You and your friend need some real medical attention or you're gonna have big problems. I'm gonna go check on the rest. Keep that leg clean, and watch over Willie for me, okay?"

I shook my head yes.

As I watched him go from prisoner to prisoner, I was grateful for what he had done for Willie and me, but I still had my suspicions. Was he really who he claimed to be? Could he have just blended into this group so easily? I suppose it's possible. There were a lot of people crammed in that hallway, and it was sort of chaotic. Where were all those Red Cross inspectors he mentioned? Hard to believe they'd just disappear. Then again, if the Krauts were able to get them inside, it would explain our mad dash to this train. They sure wouldn't want a group of inspectors seeing us or asking us questions, especially Willie.

I leaned back against the wall and settled in, listening to the rhythm of the wheels on the tracks. Where were they taking us?

I felt something brush against my sleeve, and looked down to see Willie reaching out to me. The look of pure fear was still in his eyes. I reached out and he grabbed my hand, holding onto it tightly. I noticed wounds on his wrist that looked as if he'd been chained up. I can't imagine what they put him through. I held his hand between mine and slid closer to him.

"It's okay now. We've left that place," I said.

I watched Leon continue to tend to the other prisoners. Either he is incredibly lucky or he is another damn Kraut rat sent along to get information.

Either way, I'm still keeping my damn mouth shut.

CHAPTER FOURTEEN

I'm Just Visiting for a While

November 4, 1944
Barth, Germany

"How's that leg?" I heard someone say.

I opened my eyes and saw Leon tending to Willie. I must have dozed off again. Seems that's all I've been doing lately. I'm trying to stay warm while sweating half to death, but all I really want to do is sleep. I licked my dry, cracked lips and looked around, listening to the rhythm of the clickety-clack of the train on the tracks.

"Still hurts like hell," I said. My voice sounded crackily and different. "How the hell long have we been on this train?" I asked.

"The sun just came up. Today is the ninth day," Leon answered. "Lemme take a look at that leg," he said, pulling my pants down to my knees.

I noticed the swelling had gone down a bit. Leon carefully removed the bandage and looked at my wound. It still looked pretty disgusting, but a lot better than the last time I'd seen it. Leon took his flask out and poured the last few drops on the only clean spot left on my bandage and tied it back around my leg.

"This old rot-gut seems to be helping," he said, putting the flask back in his pocket. "But that was the last of it. Hope we get where were going soon. That fever of yours is getting worse."

I looked down at Willie, who was laying very still beside me with his eyes closed.

"How's he doin'?" I asked.

"He's still alive… barely," Leon answered.

Leon settled in beside Willie and leaned against the wall of the boxcar, letting out a long sigh. He looked exhausted. I had my doubts a Kraut rat would have done so much for all of us.

"Thanks for takin' care of us," I said.

He sat motionless with his eyes closed, saying nothing.

"You really did sneak right out of that hellhole?" I asked.

"You think I coulda made up a story like that?" he asked.

"Ya gotta admit, it does sound like a line of shit. Either that, or you are the luckiest son of a bitch I've ever met," I said.

"Was that place really that bad?" he asked.

"It was run by three S.S. Death Heads who were hell-bent on torture. And that older, balding Gestapo officer that was by the train… " I said, reshuffling my weight and pulling my pants up.

"Yeah. What about him?" Leon asked.

"First time I met him, he was posing as a friendly Red Cross doctor from Nebraska. Before I knew it, I had told him a lot more than I should have. Take my advice—don't say any more than you have to to anyone. They can be pretty sneaky," I said.

"Is that why you clammed up so fast? You thought I was a… "

"I wasn't sure… and you started askin' me the same things he was. I wasn't gonna be fooled again, and still won't," I responded.

We sat in silence, listening to the sound of the wheels on the tracks below us.

"I wonder where they're taking us… " Leon asked.

I wondered the same thing. If his story about seeing Red Cross inspectors was true, it appeared we were being taken some place out of sight and as far away from Pickhardt as possible. The train began to slow down. Leon stood up and looked out the air vent on the side of the car.

"We're coming into a town," he said.

I could hear people talking outside and dogs barking as the train screeched to a stop. Not another round of running through the dogs, I hoped. I heard the door's mechanism turn and the door opened sending bright light streaming into the boxcar. Two German soldiers with rifles came in the boxcar and looked at us.

"Stehen Sie auf!" one of them shouted.

We all got up and began to walk out of the car, except for Willie, who laid motionless in the back of the car.

"Get a keilrahmen!" another of the soldiers yelled, looking at Willie.

Outside the train, two German Officers and several German soldiers, some with German Sheperds on short leashes, stood in front of a small, weathered depot building. On the front of the building was a large wooden sign painted black with gold letters that read BARTH. Beyond the train depot was a huge church with a steeple that seemed to touch the sky. Two German soldiers rushed past us carrying a stretcher into the boxcar. Others soldiers gathered the rest of us into two rows in front of the train. A small town was just beyond the church. Two German officers and a group of German soldiers stood like statues in front of us. Some of the soldiers had huge dogs at their side attached to short leashes.

The two soldiers rushed from the box car, carrying Willie past us. They loaded him in an ambulance and sped toward the town. A third and highly decorated officer paced back and forth in front of us, looking us over. I looked at the soldiers with dogs on leashes. The dogs were eying us intently, as if ready to pounce. When the train began to pull away from the station, I thought of the arrival at Tychow and the hell I went through there. Were we going to face the same thing? I hoped not. I didn't have the strength to run. I glanced around me and tried to develop a plan to stay out of danger, should he give the order to turn them loose.

"Velcome to Stalug Luft One!" the officer shouted.

I jumped when he said the word welcome. He continued to pace in front of us.

"As of zhis day, you are all preezoners auf var. You are to do vhat my men eenstruct you to do. Zhey are in charge now," he said, turning and pointing at his soldiers. "Zhey vill take you to vhere you vill be processed. For you, der var ist over!

When he finished, he walked over to the other officers and said something in German under his breath. I watched as the soldiers moved toward us without turning the dogs loose. I breathed a sigh of relief while we all began to march toward the town.

We went through an ancient looking stone wall that had to be about 100 feet tall with a narrow arched opening that led into town and down the main street past two-story buildings that housed various stores and shops on the first floor. Shop owners and workers stood in front of the stores and watched us go by. Others leaned out the windows of the second floor and watched us as well. A huge fenced in area with evenly spaced guard towers loomed ahead of us. A large pine forest stood on the right side of the compound and a vast body of water was on the left side and beyond it as far as I could see.

The smell of pine mixed with the sea air and wood smoke as we were led past a long section of fence outside the camp. A long line of worn down, haggered looking prisoners stood along the inside of the fence and watched us walk past.

"For you der var ist over!" echoed through my mind. It felt like it had just begun.

CHAPTER FIFTEEN

I Just Seen a Rat!

November 5, 1944
Stalug Luft One
Barth, Germany

"Goon up!!" I heard someone shout, making my eyes pop open. From the bottom bunk I was lying in, I noticed several American soldiers scurrying around the room, settling in and standing at attention in the center of the room just as the door burst open. A tall, lanky German soldier entered the room and began to look around. He was an odd-looking character. Big ears stuck out from the sides of his head. He had a long pointy nose and a goofy looking smile on his face. I sat up on the edge of the bed and watched him. He took long, almost cartoonish strides from bunk to bunk searching every inch. His pants were pulled halfway up his chest and the cuffs hovered just above the tops of his huge boots.

"Good afternoon, Benny," one of the soldiers said.

"'Allo, Meester Porter," he responded, still searching the bunks on the other side of the room. "I trust you are all behav-ink yourzelves… "

One of the American soldiers looked at me and motioned with his eyes and fingers for me to get up.

"Aww, you know we are, Benny. Do ya really think we'd try anything?" Porter asked.

"It's poshible." Benny said, turning around and noticing me sitting in the bed.

A couple more soldiers that were now behind Benny were

motioning me to get up with a sense of urgency.

"Vhy ees dees man still zitting down?" he asked, walking toward me.

"I just woke up, that's why," I sneered.

"Get out auf zat bed!! Rausch!!" he shouted at me.

I stood up quickly, and as Benny searched my bed, I noticed my leg didn't hurt as much as it had been. The swelling had gone down too. I rubbed the back of my head and felt a bandage over the wound there.

Benny finished rummaging through my bed and walked over to a small homemade stove made of bricks with a tin can chimney that stood in the corner of the room. He lifted the lid on a large pot that was simmering on top. Steam slowly drifted out and a wonderful smell filled the room. My stomach let out a long rumbling growl.

"You don't think we'd be hidin' something in our food, do ya Benny?" a soldier asked.

"It's poshible," he responded, sticking a finger in the pot, then to his mouth for a taste. "Vell, every zing zeems to be in order here," Benny said, walking slowly toward the door.

"Just one more zing… " he said, stopping and turning around. "Vhat ees ziss goon zing you calls me?"

"Why, that is slang for a very important person, Benny!" a tall soldier with wavy black hair told him. "You are important, ain't ya, Benny?"

Benny stood proudly in the middle of the room with a big smile, showing his remaining three teeth.

"It's poshible," he said, turning around and strutting out the door.

When the door shut, the soldiers began to snicker and relax. The tall soldier with black hair walked toward me and stuck his hand out.

"Glad to see ya up and around. I'm Joe Caporaso, from Jersey," he said as I shook his hand. "That there is Roscoe Hayes, he's from Indiana," he said, pointing toward a stocky young man, who was stirring the pot on the stove. Roscoe smiled and waved at me.

"Sidney Porter," another soldier said, holding out his hand. "I'm from Illinois... nice ta meet 'cha."

"Kenny Paulsen. I'm from North Dakota." another soldier said from across the room, straightening up a bed Benny had ransacked.

"Walt Spindler. Sullivan, Missouri." yet another said while he tidied up his bunk.

"There's a few more of us here. Robert Pulde, Ray Provost, and another new guy... came in same time as you. Leon something. They're out gettin' thier bread ration," Joe said. "That Leon fella said you were in pretty rough shape when ya came in. You've been in that bed for two days. We were startin' to wonder about you."

"I guess so. I don't remember a lot of it," I said. "I'm Jack Glide. I'm from Detroit. Where the hell am I?"

"You are in Barth, Germany. Stalag Luft One," Joe told me, offering me a cigarette.

"Thanks," I said, shielding Joe's out-stretched lighter and taking a long drag. "What day is it?"

"November Eighth," Joe said.

"What's up with that Benny guy? He all there?"

"He's one of the guards. He was doing a random inspection," Joe told me. "Don't let his appearances fool ya. He may not be the smartest fella, but he has the eyes of an eagle, the nose of a bloodhound, and the memory of an elephant. If he finds anything, it's straight to solitary. Trust me, ya don't wanna go there."

I thought of the long stint I had already done in solitary. It was an experience I wasn't looking forward to repeating.

"So what brings ya here, Jack?" Sidney Porter asked.

"A long stretch of rotten luck," I said, taking another long drag on my cigarette.

"Where'd ya go down?"

"Over Beilefeld," I told him. "My Fort' blew into pieces and I was thrown from it. Far as I know, only two of us survived. Since then, I've been passed from one Death Head to another. What's it like here?"

"I can think of a lot of places I'd rather be, but, as far as prison camps go, it's not too bad." Joe said. The rest nodded their heads in agreement. "We have to be outside for inspection and a head count every morning at 0500, again at 1300, then once more 2000. Lights out is at 2100. We take turns doin' the chores around here. The Krauts give us twelve potatoes each every week, along with a loaf of bread. Occasionally, they also give us cabbage, beets, colarabi, and turnips. We get some cheese and other stuff too, but not often. There's a library with a few books that we've all read a thousand times and a group of prisoners put on plays at a makeshift theater in the north compound. There is a full bird colonel that's a prisoner here. He is our liaison with the Krauts in charge."

"Our what?" I asked.

"Our liaison. He deals with them to make sure we are treated fairly," Joe told me.

Treated fairly? I couldn't see that happening with Pickhardt. There, a liaison would get a bullet in his back of he was lucky. Already this place sounds better.

"Ya gotta save everything here, right down to the tin cans from your supplies. There is a very active bartering system too. Ya can get almost anything by trading. Everything else we make," Joe continued.

"Can I trade something for a ticket outta this place and a ride home?" I asked.

Joe laughed. "I did say almost anything… " he added.

The smell coming from the pot on the stove continued to fill the room. My stomach let out another long, low rumbling growl.

"Man, that smells good," I said. "All they've been feedin' me since I hit the ground is garbage."

"Well, don't let the smell fool ya. It's still garbage. Roscoe has a way of making it taste good though," Sidney said.

"I heard that!!" Roscoe shouted, still stirring the pot.

"What?! I said you make it taste good!" Sidney fired back. "The Red Cross sends us care packages once a week—when the Jerries give 'em to us—that has better stuff. You have one at the foot of your bunk," Sidney added.

I looked over and saw a wooden crate the size of a small suitcase on the floor.

"We usually pool stuff together to make a pot of something to make it go farther," Joe told me.

"Thanks," I said, sitting back on the edge of the bunk and lifting the crate up on the bed beside me.

I pried the wooden top off of it and looked at the contents. Inside the crate was a can of corned beef, salmon, coffee, pork, powdered milk, and margarine. It also had a box of raisins, biscuits, and sugar cubes, along with four packs of cigarettes, four chocolate bars, and two small bars of soap. On top of it all, was a small book with YMCA wartime log on the cover, four tri-fold postcard style note papers, and three pencils.

"So tell us… " Sidney asked, sitting on the bunk across from me. "How is the war goin' out there? We any closer to gettin' outta this joint?"

"The Brits have been bombing at night, and we've been goin' back and hittin' 'em again during the day. With non-stop bombing runs, they ain't had time to rebuild, so I'd have to assume things are in our favor," I told him.

"We hear the sound of bombs to the south if it's clear and calm out," Joe said, joining us and leaning against Sidney's bunk.

"How long you guys been here?" I asked, taking a long last

drag off of my cigarette and snubbing it out on the floor.

" A year and three months," Sidney replied.

"Nine months," Roscoe said, still stirring the pot.

"Too damn long!" Walt yelled.

"Me too!" Kenny added.

Walt and Kenny stayed close together and whispered something. Out of the corner of my eye, I saw Kenny give Walt a pair of tin cans, which he hid underneath his mattress, on the back side, near the wall.

"I've been in here just shy of two years," Joe said. "One of us, Robert Pulde, has been here two months longer than I have."

I couldn't imagine being held here for that long, and didn't like the possibility of having to do so myself.

The door flung open and two more soldiers, followed closely by Leon, entered the room carrying several loaves of bread, which they placed on a long table in the center of the room. The loaves sounded like they were frozen, or made of brick when they hit the table.

"You guys are just in time! Chow's up!" Roscoe said.

"Yeah… smells good, Roscoe," one of them said with a gravely voice.

He appeared to be a little older than the rest, looked a bit weathered, yet very fit. He smiled through what looked to be a three days' growth as he silently pointed at the floor, making sure we all saw him. The room went silent. I thought I heard something move, but it sounded like it was in the floor.

"Did ya see that?!" the soldier shouted.

"See what, Robert?" Joe asked.

"I'm tellin' ya, I seen a rat run under that bunk over there!" the soldier replied. I began to look around, but Sidney nudged me and smiled, holding his finger in front of his lips.

"Why, yes!" Sidney yelled. "I just seen him run over there!"

"There he is! Get 'em!" Joe shouted. Everyone began to run around, jump up and down, and yell at nothing while Leon and I looked dumbfounded.

As quickly as they had started jumping around, they stopped and the room fell silent again. I could hear the sounds of coughing and movement under the floor. Everyone stood perfectly still and quiet until the noises subsided.

"Robert Pulde," the soldier said, walking toward me and extending his hand.

"Jack Glide," I responded, shaking his hand. "What the hell was that all about?"

"The Krauts built these shacks two feet off the ground, so they can crawl under 'em and listen in on what we say, especially when we get new arrivals itchin' to tell how it's goin' out there," Robert explained. "We wasn't all goin' crazy... we was just gettin' rid of some damn big rats."

"Seems to have worked," I chuckled.

"Just watch what ya say for awhile," he said. "This here is Ray Prevost," he said pointing to a tall thin soldier with reddish-orange hair. Ray waved back at me.

"Of course, you already know Leon. Welcome to bein' a Kreigie."

"Welcome to what?" I asked. Robert pointed to the word Kreigsgefangenpost in bold print on the front of the post cards in my Red Cross parcel.

"That word means prisoner of war camp. Too damn hard to say, so we call each other Kreigies," he explained.

I nodded my head as I stared at the post card. At last, I could let Eileen and everyone back home know I was alive. But where do I start? How do I fit all I've been through on a one page note?

"Good to see you up," I heard someone say. I looked up to see Leon standing in front of me. "You look a lot better."

"Thanks. I feel better... all things considered," I said.

"C'mon. Let's get some food in ya," Leon said, motioning to the table where the others were gathering.

I hobbled over to the table and Roscoe placed a bowl of stew in front of me. I looked at the steaming bowl filled with corned beef, potatoes, and carrots in a dark gravy.

"Take it slow," Roscoe told me. "It's not uncommon to want to wolf down your first decent meal, but you'll just heave it back up," he added.

"Or in the case of Roscoe's cookin', your second, your third, and so on... " Sidney joked.

"Aww, pipe down!" Roscoe said. "My chow ain't kilt ya yet!"

I filled a spoon with the stew and put it in my mouth. It tasted wonderful. Definitely better than anything the Krauts have given me. I took another spoonful. Then another, savoring every bite of the first decent and warm meal I'd had since I hit the ground. Before long, I was staring into a nearly empty bowl.

"Want some bread? If you're gonna eat it, you're gonna have to soak it in that, so ya don't bust a tooth." Joe told me.

"No thanks," I replied. "I've had enough of their bread for now."

"Jack was tellin' us that the Brits have been bombing all night, and we've been bombing them all day," Joe told Robert.

"That explains all the noise we've been hearin' at night," Robert responded. "So... ya think we're winnin' this thing?" he asked.

"That's what the brass has been tellin' us. Last place we bombed was already smokin' when we got there. When we dropped our eggs, we put 'em outta business for good."

"That's good," Robert said, "I ain't spendin' another Christmas or birthday here. Been so long since I seen home, I forget what it's like." He leaned close to me and spoke quietly-

"We do have a make-shift newspaper that is printed by some

guys in the north compound here. Called the POW-WOW, short for prisoners of war, waiting on winning. It's printed on carbon paper and snuck from room to room. It ain't too bad… nothin' like firsthand accounts like yours, but it gives us a little news of what's goin' on out there. Damn Krauts don't know about it, so mum's the word."

"I've spent most of this damn war here," Robert said, leaning back and pulling a pipe out of his shirt pocket.

He filled it and lit it, taking a few quick puffs before speaking. "Three months after I was drafted, they made me a navigator on a B-24. On our first mission, we went down and I wound up here," Robert said. "Were you drafted?" he asked.

"I signed up," I answered.

"Why would anyone sign up for this?"

"Long story short—I was chasin' paradise."

"Have ya found it yet?"

I thought about the question and the circumstances that led me here. "I'm workin' on it," I told him, thinking of Eileen and back home.

"If you'll excuse me, I have a letter to write."

CHAPTER SIXTEEN

Rosary, Don't Fail Me Now

November 15, 1944
Our Lady of Good Council Church
Detroit, Michigan

"Hi, Eileen"

The words startled me. I had been so caught up in praying my rosary, I didn't see anyone coming.

"Father Lynch... I didn't see you there," I said, looking up at the young priest standing in front of me.

He has only been at our parish a few months. He always has a kind word, offers support when I am feeling down and shares my optimism that someday, good news about Jack would come.

"You were quite involved in prayer... sorry to disturb you," he responded.

"That's okay," I said, getting up from the kneeler and sitting back in the pew.

"Still no news?" he asked

"Not yet, Father..."

"How long has it been?" he asked.

"It's been a month and a half," I said, looking down, letting the rosary beads slide through my fingers.

"You're going to wear out that rosary praying as much as you have... mind if I join you?"

"Not at all, Father. Please do." I said.

He sat down next to me on the pew.

"I know you're hurting, but I hope no matter what happens,

you keep your faith," he said.

"Oh, I do have faith, Father. I know he will be alright. I'll just keep praying. I'll hear something soon."

A look of sadness came over his face as he cupped my hand in both of his.

"I am proud of your devotion, Eileen, I truly am... but... " his voice trailed off as he stared up at the altar

"But what, Father?" I asked.

"There comes a time when God tests your faith."

"My faith is as strong as it ever was, Father. I have prayed for his safety since he left for the war and I'll pray long after he comes home."

"Suppose he doesn't? It's been awhile since his plane went down."

"He will be back!" I snapped. "I just know in my heart he is alive."

"I hope you're right. Just keep in mind, everything happens for a reason, good or bad. We may not understand it or like it, but we have to trust in God's will."

"I know, Father." I realized what he was doing. He was preparing me for the worst, but I just wasn't ready to give up on Jack. I knew with each passing day, the chances of getting good news were getting slimmer, but somehow I still felt I would.

"Well, I guess I should get going, Father. The mail should be coming soon," I said, putting my rosary back in my purse.

"Remember—both of you are in my prayers. See you at mass tomorrow—and I hope you get that good news soon," he told me.

As I walked out the front door of the church a sudden stiff breeze caught me off guard, blowing my hat off. I caught it and pulled it down a little farther and began the walk home.

It was a chilly November morning, the fifteenth, which was also Jack's birthday, making the waiting all the worse. Thanksgiving and Christmas were just around the corner. It is normally my favorite time of year, but I just couldn't get into the season so far, all I wanted was news. Any news.

Shortly after we got the letter from his chaplain, we also got one from his Commanding Officer that also was an attempt to reassure us that sometimes it could take a while to hear anything and to remain optimistic. They were nice gestures, but they still didn't give the answers to questions that ran through my mind constantly. Where was he? was he okay?

I thought of what Father Lynch had told me as I walked home. The tactfully given "trust in God's will" speech he gave me meant he was losing hope. I was running out of optimists just when I needed them the most.

I thought about Jack and wondered where he could be. It had been so long and still not a single word. I didn't know if that is good or bad. No news meant they didn't recover his body where his plane went down. If they didn't find him there, he could have survived. It could also mean they never found him, or there wasn't enough left.

No. I mustn't think that way. I have to think positive.

A car horn startled me, making me realize I had almost walked right out into a busy intersection.

Maybe he has been found, I thought, waiting for the crosswalk signal. He is far from home, and, just as both letters suggested, word did take a long time to arrive. I have to cling to hope. The signal light turned green and I continued on.

A sad smile came over my face as I remembered the almost daily letters I would get from him. It seemed like forever since I'd gotten one.

"Oh… I'm so sorry," I said to a gentleman I almost walked into.

I noticed he was staring into my eyes. He was well dressed, wearing a long black overcoat, and a black Fedora hat. I could almost see myself in the shine on his black shoes. That was how I realized I was about to walk into him. I saw those shoes coming at me while I was looking down. I felt like such a klutz.

"Goot auf-ternoon," he said, tipping his hat, before continuing on his way.

I couldn't place the accent. He seemed kind of creepy.

What if everyone was right? What if I never saw Jack again? I turned onto our street and tried to picture my life without him. He just has to be okay.

"Why can't I just get some news… any news," I mumbled to myself while I continued on. "God, if you are listening, please let me know where he is, what he is… " I said, walking up the sidewalk to our house and approaching the mailbox. This was becoming a daily ordeal I dreaded, yet couldn't wait for every day.

I opened the box and took out the small stack of envelopes. I thumbed through them one by one. My heart began to sink as I went through the assortment of bills, cards and letters and still nothing.

A gust of wind suddenly came up, nearly blowing the mail out of my hands. I regathered the mail, and noticed a simple small white piece of paper folded in thirds sticking up between two brown envelopes.

The hair on my neck stood up when I pulled it out. The front of it had the underlined word Kriegsgefangenpost printed on it. My name and address was under that along with some other German words and several canceled stamps in German and French.

I dropped the mail on the porch and hurriedly opened the mysterious note. Tears ran down my cheeks as I began to read the simple one-page note that read:

How's my honey? What's she been thinkin' of? Still love me? Sure you're not lyin?

I'm writing to let you know I am alive and okay. Guess I was pretty lucky sweetheart, 'cause out of our whole crew, there are only two of us alive. I guess God was looking out for me alright 'cause I was knocked out and blown out of the ship before it went down. I came out of it with a little cut on my head, and my leg hurts, but it's not broken.

I'm allowed to write two letters and four cards a month, so you'll know I am okay and that I love you more than ever.

By the time I get out of here, I'll have quite a bit of back pay coming, so we should have a good start on our own home.

Speaking of a home, I was going to surprise you when I got back, but since I don't know how long I'll be here, I'll let you in on my secret. I've been sending most of my pay home to my dad, so we may already have enough for that house you really love. I want you to get it from him and buy it, so it will be ours when I get there.

So honey, look at it that way. We'll have a house of our own, and we'll have the rest of our lives to live.

Please don't worry about me, as I am doing just fine. I'd better tell you again I love you, but you already know that. I hope and pray the day I can come home comes soon and I'll be able to hold you in my arms again.

I'll close for now,

XOXOXOXO

Your Jack

Tears of joy streamed down my face. I sat down on the porch, leaned against the house and began to laugh and cry at the same time. He is alive!!

"Yes! Yes! YES!" I cried out.

"Good Heavens, dear!" my mother said, opening the door, seeing me sitting on the porch crying. "What happened? Did you fall down?"

"NO!" I said, holding up the note. "Jack is alive!"

"What?!" she said.

"He is alive! He sent me this note!" I said, handing it to her. A look of disbelief washed across her face as she looked at the note.

"Oh, thank God!" she shouted. I stood back up and we looked at each other with huge smiles.

"He is alive!!" we both shouted out, the sound of our voices echoing down the block.

We both began to dance in a circle on the porch, singing,

"He is alive! He is AAALLLIIIVVVEEE!!!!"

CHAPTER SEVENTEEN

A Kriegie's Life

November 9th, 1944
Stalug Luft One
Barth, Germany

"That who you was writin' to?" I heard someone ask.

I looked up to see Sidney peering over my shoulder from the bunk above mine.

"Yeah," I said still staring at the photo of Eileen.

"She's pretty. That your wife?"

"Gonna be… soon as I get home," I answered.

"Gonna let the rest of us see?" Joe asked, looking up from the book he was reading on the top bunk across from me.

I turned the picture around and showed it to Joe. The others sat up from their bunks and looked at it too.

"Damn!" I heard Robert say. "You left her behind to find your so-called paradise?"

"No. I met her after I signed up. Kind of a long story," I told them.

"We all love a good story," Joe said. "Let's hear it."

"Yeah!" Sidney said. The rest sat up on their bunks.

"Lookit I found!" Leon said, coming through the door holding a big black cat.

"I ain't feedin' no damn cat!" Roscoe yelled. "Hard enough findin' enough for us to eat around here!"

"I'll take care of him myself! He's such a friendly soul, and he seems to like me," Leon said, sitting on the bunk across from me.

The cat curled up in his lap and began to purr.

"Check out the picture of Jack's dame back home!" Sidney told him.

I turned the picture toward Leon and he let out a low whistle.

"Jack was just gonna tell us his story, wasn't ya?" Joe said.

"I guess," I said. "Where do I start?"

"On what possessed you to sign up for this shit," Robert said.

"A pretty girl, and a broken down car," I answered.

"We're listenin'… " Sidney said.

"I dropped out of school and worked in a scrap yard—Banty's in Dearborn—cuttin' up cars," I began. "There was this dame that would walk past the place and smile at me. Blonde hair, big blue eyes. Prettiest thing you ever seen."

"And?" Joe asked.

"Her name was Edwina Blount, daughter of William Blount, a successful businessman and one of the richest guys in the neighborhood," I told them. "I'da given anything to be with her, but I was just a mutt compared to her family. I didn't stand a chance. Then one day, old man Banty told me to cut up the car out back for scrap. It turned out to be a 1932 Cadillac V-16 that even had crystal vases and curtains in the back. It was a deep maroon color, with black fenders, dual side mounts, the whole nine yards. I took one look at it and came up with an idea."

"What was something like that doin' in a scrapyard?" Robert asked. "And what's got to do with this dame?"

"The radiator leaked like a sieve. And it had everything to do with her," I explained. "I made a deal with Banty to trade the car for a month of free labor. At the time, I could get a Model A Ford for a week's worth of pay. Sometimes he'd just give 'em to me. But I knew if I had that Cadillac, I could impress Edwina, and look like I was something to her family."

"Did it work?" Sidney asked.

"Yes and no," I answered. "I patched up the radiator as best I could. It still leaked a little so I put plain water in it instead of alcohol. I'd have to drain it every night so it wouldn't freeze, but I felt like a king driving that thing. I offered Edwina a ride home one cold November day, and even talked her into going to a show with me on my eighteenth birthday."

"Sounds good so far. What happened?" Joe asked.

"It was very cold when I picked her up and light snow was falling. She looked great. She was wearing a fancy blue dress and a mink stole around her neck. Her perfume smelled delightful as she walked past me while I held the car door open for her. I made a good impression with her dad too. We laughed and talked all the way to the theater, basking in the warmth of the comfy heater," I said. "Tell the truth, I don't even remember what picture was showing that night. I had my arm around a beautiful girl. She was enjoying my company. I had it made. I could see myself gettin' a cushy job from old man Blount and never havin' to stand out in the cold, freezin' my ass off, cuttin' up scrap again."

"Then what happened?" Robert asked.

"When the show was over, we walked arm in arm back to my car, enjoying the falling snow. She slid in close to me when we got in the car. I turned on the ignition and hit the starter button. Nothing."

"Uhh ohh… " Sidney said.

"She asked what was wrong and began to shiver," I explained. "I thought that maybe the battery was dead. I switched on the lights and they burned bright, eliminating that possibility. I told her I'd check it out and when I opened the hood, I noticed a huge crack the entire length of the engine block."

"Not good," Leon said.

"Yeah. That car wasn't goin' anywhere 'cept back to Banty's yard to be scrapped," I told them. "The worst part was I had to confess to my date I didn't have any money left for a cab or a trolley.

104

We had to walk four blocks to a pay phone so she could call her dad. By the time he got there and put his frozen daughter in his car, he was furious. He told me if he caught me anywhere near his daughter, there would be hell to pay. From the look on her face, it didn't appear that it was going to be a problem."

"That's what led you sign up for the war," Robert asked.

"I didn't exactly sign up for the war. The date was November 15, 1941. I was walkin' home and went past a recruitment office. I saw a picture of a huge silver airplane in the window. Under the picture the sign said join the Army Air Corps and see the world." I lit up a cigarette and leaned against the side of my bunk.

"When I was a kid, my mom used to show me pictures of far off exotic places in magazines," I said, pausing to take a long drag and a slow exhale. "I was eighteen and still walkin' around Detroit. I figured the Air Corps was the only way I was ever gonna see any of those places, so I signed up. How was I to know the goddamn Japs were gonna bomb Pearl a few weeks later."

"Did ya get to see any of those fancy places?" Leon asked, stroking the mane of the sleeping cat in his lap.

"Not a one of 'em," I answered. "But I did see a lot of places in the U.S. during my training period. My friend Mike and I had a lot of fun going from place to place." I reminisced.

"Was he a part of your crew?" Joe asked.

"Naw. He turned out to be a damn good fighter pilot. Our training began at a slow pace, but they soon needed soldiers all over the world right away. Whatever you were good at at the moment, was what you were assigned to do. He went to Italy to fly P-51's. I wound up bein' a radio operator in a B-17 based in England," I said.

Joe turned to look out the window. "Looks like the goon's are bringin' us a new roomie!"

Everyone leapt to their feet. Leon stuffed the cat under his bunk just before the door opened. I couldn't believe my eyes when

I seen two German soldiers escort Willie Strong into our room and guide him to a bunk on the other side of the room.

"I'll be damned," Leon muttered. "I'd written him off for dead. How the hell did he survive?"

"You guys know him?" Robert asked as the soldiers left the room.

"He wound up goin' to the same hellish place they sent me to at first. It was a POW camp run by three Death Heads that specialized in torture," I said. "They really worked him over bad."

"What the hell kinda place did they send you to?" Robert asked.

"The worst place on earth. Given the chance, I'd kill all three of those bastards in charge, and not lose a minute of sleep over it. The only reason any of us that came from there are alive is because they had to hide us from Red Cross inspectors," I said.

"Makes this place sound like the Hilton," Sidney chuckled.

We all looked over toward Willie who was lying in his bunk, motionless, staring straight up the bottom of the bunk above him.

"So where is this paradise you think you've found?" Robert asked.

I held up the picture of Eileen again.

"Fair enough," Robert said.

"You're one lucky man, Jack," Joe added, lying back in his bunk and picking his book back up.

I took a drag from my cigarette and watched the smoke slowly drift upwards with my exhale. I could have gone down with the others in the Purple Heart, but was lucky enough to be spared. I was lucky enough to take a bullet in the leg, rather than somewhere else. God knows what those Death Heads that thought I was Jewish would have done to me if the Red Cross hadn't showed up. I looked over at Willie, who would likely never be the same, and wondered if I would have met the same fate eventually.

But, I was also a million miles from home, injured, a prisoner in Nazi Germany, and God knows how long I'd be stuck here. Tell me again—where was the lucky part?

I looked over at Leon sitting on his bunk with his cat on his lap. Both of them looked pretty happy and content.

"I think I'll call you Lucky," Leon said to the cat, stroking its fur.

"Of course," I mumbled. "What else could you possibly call him."

CHAPTER EIGHTEEN

Happy Days Are Here Again

November 18, 1944
Detroit, Michigan

"Happy days are here again..." I sang to myself while walking to work. On top of hearing from Jack, the first snow of the season started this morning. To me, there is nothing quite like the first snow. It's so white and pure... like a new beginning in a way.

I stopped and stuck my tongue out, catching a few ice cold snowflakes. Jack and I will have our new beginning and start our lives together when he gets back home. There is an extra spring in my step as I walk along and think of the day that will happen. I know that there is uncertainty as to when, but at least I know that it will happen.

"The skies above are clear again... let's sing a song of cheer again..." I continued to sing. A layer of the whitest snow I've seen covered everything. Getting good news meant I could enjoy my favorite time of year. Soon I would have my dream house too.

"Your cares and troubles are gone... there'll be no more from now on... happy days are here..." I hummed, stopping short as I approached the front door of the lumber yard. Across the street, the same guy I almost walked into a few days ago was standing under the awning of the five and dime, looking at me. Who is that?

A panel truck screeched to a stop at the curb, blocking the view of across the street. The lettering on the side read H. Humprey Jones, est. 1939. When the horn sounded, I looked at the driver, noticing it was Jack's dad.

"Hi ya Red!" he said, crawling out the passenger door.

"Hey!... Pops?" I said, feeling that 'Mr. Glide' was starting too sound to formal, but unsure just what to call him.

"Pops?" he asked. "I kinda like the sound'a that!"

"Beautiful day, isn't it?" I asked, opening the front door and holding it open. I glanced across the street from the steps of the lumber yard and noticed the mysterious stranger was gone.

"It sure is, Red. And good for business," he said.

"Business?" I asked. Had he gotten a job? That would explain him driving that truck.

"The insulation business," he said, walking into the store.

"Did you get a job doing that?" I asked.

"Better'n that," he said. "I own the business."

"I don't understand," I said, setting my purse on the counter by the cash register.

"I got a chance to get in on something big, Red," he said under his breath, handing me a swatch of fluffy pale yellow material that looked like cotton candy. "Fiberglass insulation is gonna be the next big thing. They actually came up with the stuff to insulate airplanes, just like Jack's. Hell, it keeps out the cold even at forty below! Think about it, Red. The stuff will save folks a lot of money on heating oil. With the war goin' on and oil bein' rationed, what you have will go much farther. If we use less, more can go to the war effort. They'll be spendin' less, and helpin' win the war. It'll start out as a patriotic thing to do, but when folks see how good this stuff is, and it will be big even after the war. I'm tellin' ya, Red, this is gonna be a gold mine!"

Of all of the schemes I'd seen him come up with, this one actually seemed to make sense.

"I already got two houses to do, an' I'm just gettin' started," he told me.

"That's great!" I said. I really hoped this venture would pay off

109

for him. He really deserved something to go his way.

"So, how ya doin', Red? Was great hearin' from the boy, wasn't it?" he asked.

"It was the best thing to ever happen to me Pops. I did a lot of praying and hoping, but even I was beginning to wonder. But now I know he is okay. Now I know he'll be coming home again, hopefully soon, and we'll have our life together... in our own home," I said, dropping a subtle hint.

"Yeah. He told me about that," he said, clearing his throat. "Listen, this opportunity came up sorta sudden, see, and I had to jump at it right away..." he said nervously. "Here's the thing... I hadda use his money to get in on it... but I'll have it back to ya in no time."

"Oh... okay," I said, wondering if it would be soon enough to buy the house.

"Well, I'm off to work, Red... gotta get ya that house! Don't you worry 'bout a thing... you'll see," he said opening the door and stepping out into the snow.

Through the window, I watched him get in the old panel truck and drive off. I hoped he could make good on his promise, but wondered about his latest venture. It all sounds great, but what if it doesn't take off like he said? All too often, things seemed to go south when it came to big ideas, but I knew in my heart he'd do his best. How do I break the news to Jack?

I really love that house, but when it all boils down, it's only boards and bricks. I'll still have Jack.

CHAPTER NINETEEN

A New Arrival

November 27,1944
Stalug Luft One
Barth, Germany

I watched my cigarette smoke drift upward from my mouth and crawl slowly around the boards on the bunk above me. The soft curls of smoke seemed to follow the grain of the wood, silently creeping to the edge of the bunk, before free floating out across the room.

Willie began to stir in his bunk. He rolled onto his back and opened his eyes. He and I were the only ones in the room.

"How ya doin', Willie?" I asked.

"Where are we?" he said quietly, looking around the room.

"We're in Barth, Germany," I told him.

I walked over and sat on the bunk across from him.

"Good to see ya doin' better. This place seems a lot better than where we were."

He slowly sat up on the edge of his bed and looked around. I shook a cigarette slightly out of my pack and offered it to him. He still had a look of fear in his eyes.

"I ain't never had one a 'dose," he told me.

"When I got to England I was pretty nervous 'bout flyin' into combat," I told him. "A doctor recommended 'em to calm my nerves. Seems to work."

Willie took the cigarette from the pack and put it in his mouth. I held my lighter out and lit it for him. He took a big puff and started coughing violently.

"Breathe through your mouth and take a slower drag on it. Then slowly let it out," I told him.

He took another puff and watched the smoke flow out of his mouth and float away.

"Thanks," he said, taking another drag, then sitting silently.

"What part of Detroit are ya from?" I asked.

"Porter Street... just off of Trumbull," Willie answered.

"No kiddin'? My dad had a campground and store on Fort Street. Right across from the Rouge Plant. I used to walk to Navin Field and watch the Tigers play," I told him.

"Me too!" Willie said. "We was dirt floor poor, an' I never had no money. But I got pretty good at sneakin' in... " he added.

"Same here! I got caught one time, and was actually able to bullshit my way into bein' a bat boy for a season."

Willie laughed and displayed a big smile of pearl white teeth that contrasted brightly against his dark skin. It looked like he was starting to come out of the shell Pickhardt had put him in.

"How did you do that?" he asked.

"I think they caught me so many times they were beginnin' to feel sorry for me," I chuckled.

Willie laughed, but soon seemed wary again, and kept looking around the room.

"So, what's your story? How'd ya wind up here?" I asked.

"I was based in Ramitelli, Italy... part of the 332th," Willie explained. "I flew P-51's as escort for B-17's over Germany, mostly. I was on my tenth mission when I got hit and had to bail out."

"Where did ya have to bail out?" I asked.

"Over Beilefeld," Willie answered. "Ever been there?"

"Hell yeah!" I said. "That's where my Fort got blown up! When did ya go down?"

"September 30th," Willie said, exhaling a plume of smoke. "It was a day I'll never forget. It was the day my time in hell began."

"Same day, same destination for me," I sighed. "You was a member of the Red Tails? Gonna send a thank you note to ole Eleanor?"

"That I was. Seen some heavy combat… but, I ain't never been so scared in all my days… " Willie said, dropping his cigarette on the floor and snubbing it out. "I keep expecting to see the devil come back through that door," he confessed. "An' Eleanor can kiss my black ass… "

"I know what ya mean," I told him. "But, I ain't seen anybody like those blood thristy bastards there. And I got your back if anyone tries anything. We're from Detroit… we're tough, right?"

"I always thought I was. I just didn't know how much. Till now," Willie said.

The door flung open and Willie jumped in fear, sliding himself to the back of his bunk against the wall. Leon and Robert Pulde entered the room carrying the potato ration for the week.

"Here's a couple of our roommates now," I said. "Guys, say hello to my friend Willie here."

Leon and Robert walked over and extended their hands.

"Robert Pulde. Nice to see ya up and movin,' Willie."

"Leon Swisher. Glad to finally meet ya," he said.

"Leon took care of us on the train ride here. Probably saved both our hides," I told Willie.

He slowly slid back away from the wall and shook both of their hands.

"I'm just glad you made it. Damn Krauts really roughed you up… " Leon told him.

Willie shook his head yes. The look in his eyes suggested he was trying hard not to think about it.

"Hey! Mind if I take these?" Robert asked Willie, pointing at some strips of wood peeling from the side of Willies bunk.

Willie moved aside and shook his head yes again.

"There's a guy over in the North Compound buildin' a violin from scratch. He could use 'em," Robert explained.

"He's buildin' a what?" I asked.

"A violin," Robert told us. "He knows how to play, and makin' one passes the time. Also keeps his mind offa things."

I knew the feeling. Anything you can do to keep busy helps. Other than books from the library or seein' a play, there isn't much to do. Some whittle things from chunks of scrap wood, or melt tin foil to sculpt things like model airplanes. Leon has his cat to keep him busy. I've taken to drawing pictures and coming up with short rhymes to keep my mind off of the minutes dragging by. I can't imagine a homemade violin sounding like much, but if it passes time, why not?

"Hey guys!" Joe Caparosa yelled, flinging the door open and making Willie jump again. "There is a new batch of prisoners comin' in!"

"C'mon, lets go!" Robert said.

He and Leon started walking to the door.

"Wanna go see?" I asked Willie. "It's the most exciting thing going on around here, and ya never know; ya may see someone you know."

Willie stirred in his bed, staring at the floor. I lit up a cigarette and offered him one.

"C'mon," I said lighting his cigarette. "Do ya good to get some fresh air, don'cha think?" I asked.

Willie shrugged his shoulders and exhaled a plume of smoke.

"You may be right," He responded. We got up and walked out the barrack, buttoning our coats and pulling up our collars. Dark clouds hung over the Baltic Sea. A stiff wind was coming on shore giving the air a crisp bite.

Other prisoners stared at Willie as we walked toward the fence at the entry of the compound. I could see some pointing at him and saying things I couldn't make out. Willie just walked along, looking straight ahead.

"Now they're lettin' niggers in here?" A prisoner sneered as we walked past him.

"You gotta problem with my friend, pal?" I turned and asked him, standing face to face with him.

"What's it to ya?" he asked me. "An' I ain't your pal… especially if you hang around with darkies," he said, pointing at Willie.

"Leave him alone… or you'll be answerin' to me," I hissed.

"Oooo! Tough guy!" he said, holding his hands up and walking away.

I could hear him making snide remarks while Willie and I walked up to the fence. We stood in awkward silence watching the rows of new prisoners approaching from the edge of town. I thought about the things that prisoner said about Willie. Back in Detroit, it wouldn't have been all that uncommon for me or my friends to refer to a black man a Jig-a-boo or a Spook. Back home, Willie would have had his world, and I'd have had mine, but here, Willie was just another survivor, same as me.

"You shouldn'ta oughta done that… " Willie told me.

"Done what?" I asked.

"Made sumpin' outta what that guy said 'bout me. I's been livin' wit that all my life. Best thing ta do is jus' keep on walkin'," he said.

"I'm not much for walkin' away," I said, watching the new arrivals start to file past us.

Leon, Joe, and Robert joined us, standing along the fence, watching the weary faces pass by.

"Good God! Leon said. "Lookit that poor guy!"

A tall, thin soldier wearing a flight jacket with pilots wings walked past that made us all wince. His face was burned beyond recognition, his eyelids and upper lip hung limp on his face. Parts of his flight goggles were burned into his face. An awful stench of burned flesh hung in the air when he passed in front of us.

"Man. I feel sorry for him," Joe said. The pilot suddenly turned toward us, looked straight at me, and stopped walking.

"Shh-hh… shh-hh… " he said.

His face looked like something out of a horror movie.

"Bewegen Sie sich!" A German soldier told him shoving him from behind. The pilot started walking again, but he continued to turn back and stare at me.

"You know him?" Robert asked.

"Never seen him before in my life," I answered.

"He sure seemed to notice you," Joe said.

I looked at him again and tried to think if I had seen him before. Maybe he was someone from Debach? I didn't recognize him, but new crews came in just about every day. Why was he telling me to shh? I wasn't saying anything. The others were. Who the hell was that guy?

Seeing him triggered memories of Malloy bring ripped from the Purple Heart and the piece of his burned flesh I found stuck to my jacket when I hit the ground. I remembered clowning around with him and the rest of the crew the morning we went down.

"You okay?" I heard Willie ask.

"Yeah. I was just remembering a good friend," I replied.

When the last of the new prisoners walked past, we began to walk back to the barracks and I pondered the fate of my crew. What, or who, determines who lives and who dies? I reached the barracks, entered, and sat in silence on my bunk with visions of Malloy still running through my mind like a raging river. After awhile, I picked up my YMCA log book and began to write,

They say he died in glory,
Whatever that may be.
If it's dying in a burst of flame,
Then glory's not for me.
In the briefing room this morning,
He sat with clear eyes and a strong heart,
Just one of many airmen
Determined to do his part.
My buddy had the guts alright,
He sought not glory nor fame.
He knew there was a job to do,
My crew all felt the same.
But death had the final word,
In it's log it wrote his name.
For my buddy died this afternoon,
In glory—in a burst of flame.

CHAPTER TWENTY

What Did You Call Me?

November 29, 1944
Stalug Luft One
Barth, Germany

"So, what is your story, Joe?" I asked as we gathered our potato ration from the pile.

"Not much to tell, really," Joe said. "I grew up on the Jersey shore. We never had much, so when I got drafted, I figured, what the hell, least I'd be eatin' regular," Joe explained, placing the last of our potatoes in the cart.

"How'd ya wind up here?" I asked.

"I was assigned to the 482nd Bombardment Group as a tail gunner on a B-17. We were shot down on our first mission. We were having a hell of a time lining up our target. Wound up doubling back to try again… that was when we got waxed."

"Didn't have the Norden bomb sight then?" I asked.

We were one of the first to get one, which allowed the bombardier to steer the plane from his position rather than tell the pilot which way to go.

"Naw. It was the first part of the war, and before we had that," Joe explained. "Lotta crews were lost having to double back. Pretty tough to line up a target with someone else doin' the steerin'. We had to bail and I've been here ever since."

"The rest of your crew make it out too?" I asked.

"We lost our side gunner and bombardier. Both of em got shot."

A vision of the Purple Heart going down ran through my mind. I thought of all of my crew members that never made it.

"How 'bout your crew?" Joe asked.

"Just me an our engineer made it. Something ran into us. I think we survived simply because we were tossed from the plane. The others never had time to bail," I said while we slogged through the newly fallen snow.

"Too bad... " Joe said, positioning the cart in front of our barracks door.

"Hell of a way to go... " I said, propping the door open, so we could unload the cart.

The others began to help carry the potatoes and put them in the bin inside.

"The mail came while you guys were out. You got a letter Jack," Leon told me.

"From who?!" I asked.

Judging from the writing, and the smell of perfume, I'd have to say it's from your dame back home," Leon answered.

This was the moment I had been waiting for! I hurried through unloading the potatoes and went over to my bunk, sitting on the edge, staring at the envelope, taking in the lilac scented perfume that permeated the paper.

She must have gotten my note and responded. I couldn't wait to see the letter. I tore the envelope open and sat on my bunk and began to read:

> Sweetheart,
>
> I can't tell you how happy I was to get your note and finally know that you are okay! Everyone here has been praying for you since we heard your plane went down. I want you to know I love you more

than ever, and can't wait till you can come home. Hopefully SOON!

I was so sorry to hear about the rest of your crew, but am so happy you survived. I can't imagine my life without you. What is wrong with your leg? You said it's hurt, but not broken?

What is it like there? I've so many questions, but I just worry about you sweetheart. Don't worry about me, I'll be just fine, now that I know you're okay. I miss you and love you so so much that I am walking on air since I got your note!

I laughed when I heard about your surprise. I've been saving for that house too! My dad did check on the house, and found out it was sold anyway. None of that matters to me, sweetheart. All that matters is that we will have the rest of our lives to live happily ever after; where doesn't matter one bit.

Oh, and your dad has started a new business insulating houses and it really seems to be going well for him. He did have to use some of your money to start it, but don't be sore with him though honey, his heart was in the right place, and he is paying it back. In fact, he says the business is yours when you get home.

Please stay safe and remember I love you!

Your Eileen XOXOXOXOXO

"He did WHAT?!" I yelled out.

"What's wrong?" Willie and Leon asked.

"My old man spent the money I was savin' to buy my gal a house on one of his big ideas!" I shouted. "I can't believe this!! How could he!!"

I stood up and paced back and forth.

"I'm stuck over here an' he's pissin' away my life!" I screamed out.

"Calm down Jack," Willie said, standing up and putting his hand on my back.

"I'm goin' for a Goddamn walk." I fumed, grabbing my jacket and storming out the door.

Once outside, I lit up a cigarette and started walking. To where, I didn't know. I wished I could walk right out of here and all the way to Detroit.

The nerve of that guy, I mumbled to myself. An' I can have the business when I get back. My damn luck there will be no business an' no damn money either!

I stomped through the snow toward the fence surrounding the camp. I couldn't really go anywhere, so I figured I'd just walk around the perimeter till I simmered down.

"Shh-shh… shh-shh… " I heard someone say.

I turned around to see that badly burned pilot walking behind me, holding out his hand. I could smell that awful stench of burned flesh again.

"Not a good time to be shushin' me, buddy," I said, walking along the fence line.

I could here footsteps behind me and every time I looked over my shoulder, there he was. I just can't shake this damn guy. What the hell does he want with me? I started walking faster, quickly cutting around a building before cutting back to the fence line. It seemed to work; I didn't see or smell him anymore.

I stopped at a spot along the fence facing the Baltic Sea and stood there, watching some lazy snow-covered waves slowly lap against the shore. Some old row boats were laying upside down in the sand near the water. I wanted to burst through the fence, run to a boat, paddle to the other side and be in Switzerland. I'd figure out how to get home from there. In my mind, I heard Eileen's voice say "Please stay safe, and remember I love you."

I chuckled thinking about my fool-hardy idea to escape and tossed my cigarette in the snow, listening to it hiss till it died out. She was right. Our life together was all that really mattered. We'd find another house. But, from now on, I'm having my pay sent to her. I'd deal with dad once I got out of this place.

"Shh-shh… shh-shh… " I heard from behind me.

Jesus Christ! This guy sure is persistent, whoever he is. I turned around and there he was; a sad look on his face and an out stretched hand. He sure had more problems than me, bein' all burned to hell. Maybe he just needs a friend.

"Do I know you?" I asked.

"Shh-shhh… " he said, obviously having a hard time talking because of his burns. I waited while he tried to speak again.

"Shh-shh-orr," he said, pointing at me. I looked at the Baltic shoreline, then back at him.

"The shore?" I asked, pointing to the Sea.

"Nnn-nn-oo," he said, visibly irritated with his speech. "Shh-shh-orr… ttt… Shh-orr-t-t-ee… " he stuttered, pointing at me. "I-i-i-t Mmm-mmm… "

"Shorty? Did you just call me Shorty?" I asked. He shook his head yes wildly, then pointed to himself.

"I-i-t mmm-mm-eee! Mmm-ike!"

"Mike?!" I shouted in astonishment. Tears began to stream down his face. He shook his head yes and tried to smile.

"Holy shit! Is it really you?" I asked. He stood there, arms limp at his sides, crying like a baby.

"Y-y-yea," he said. I didn't know what to say. I was ashamed of myself for not recognizing him. What the hell happened to him? I put my arms around him and held him tight while he sobbed.

"It's alright, buddy," I told him. "C'mon. Let's get you inside and get you some help."

122

Mike Postek
Basic Training, Jefferson Barracks, MO

CHAPTER TWENTY ONE

Don't Sit Under the Apple Tree

November 25th, 1944
Detroit, Michigan

"This just in! Armed Forces Radio reports that French troops have taken over the town of Stratsbourg yesterday, thereby bringing another loss to the Nazi regime… " echoed from the radio behind the counter in the lumber yard.

"Yes!" I shouted. That was great news. Last week we heard that the gas chambers in Auschwitz had been shut down for good. The week before, a whole unit of German soldiers surrendered in the town of Aachen. With each bit of good news, it looked as if the war was being won by the allies, which made the chances of Jack coming home soon better each day.

"Got a minute Eileen?" I heard someone say.

I turned to see my boss, John Putnam standing next to me. "Sure! What's up Mr. P?" I said.

"We have the chance to make some serious money with a new customer," he explained. "He is into several businesses in Detroit, and just bought the old Book-Cadillac hotel and wants to spruce it up a bit."

"That's great Mr. P!" I answered.

"I want you to make sure he is very happy doing business here. Keep an eye on his purchases, make sure we get them to him right away. Maybe even suggest some other purchases, if you can," he told me.

"I'd be glad to Mr. P. Who is it?"

"It's none other than the William Blount," he told me.

The name sounded familiar, but I couldn't place it.

"I will do my best," I told him.

"Good. I have a lot of confidence in you Eileen," he told me. "He should be in later. Can you give him a tour? See what all he is looking to buy?"

"I sure will," I said.

I hoped I could live up to his hopes. Selling enough stuff to restore the Book-Cadillac could mean a small fortune for the store.

"Hi Ya Red!" I heard Pops say.

"Hi Pops! How are you today?"

"Finer than frog hair Red," He said. "Lookit I got in the mail." I looked at the telegram he was holding and began to read to myself.

Dear Mr. Glide;

As of yet, we have not received any news in regards to whereabouts of your son, Jack K Glide. I have every confidence that I shall be hearing something in the very near future.

I ask that you continue to keep the faith and your hopes high.

I have included Sgt. Glide, as well as others who are listed as missing in action, in my daily prayers for their safety and well being.

I assure you, the moment I hear any news, I will forward it to you immediately.

Sincerely,

James T. McCarthy, Captain
Group Chaplain

"He doesn't know yet?!" I gasped.

"Apparently not," Pops chuckled. "Think you can let him know?"

"I'd be glad to!" I said.

Over his shoulder, I could see that creepy guy standing on the sidewalk across the street. He was staring directly at me again.

"Thanks Red!" Pops said. "I gotta get off to work… busy busy busy!"

"Hey Pops… " I said. "You ever seen that guy before?" I asked, pointing across the street.

The man saw both of us looking at him, turned away, and began to walk down the street.

"Not that I recall. Why?" Pops asked.

"This is the third time I've seen him. I almost walked right into him the other day. Has a strange accent and a creepy way about him… It's pry nothing," I said.

"He is dressed pretty fancy for down here," Pops said.

"Maybe that's it. He just looks out of place, I guess," I said.

"Who knows Red," Pops said. "I'm off to work… see ya later!"

"Bye Pops." I said, noticing a well dressed man coming in the store followed by a young lady about the same age as me.

He was wearing a custom tailored suit, with a fancy overcoat with a black fur collar. Expensive looking rings were on nearly every finger. An expensive looking silk hat sat tilted on his head. The young lady with him also looked to be wearing a custom tailored blue dress and a luxurious mink coat. A fancy string of pearls was draped around her neck, and fancy diamond earrings dangled on her ears. A fancy hat that matched her dress covered her long blonde hair. She had piercing big blue eyes.

"Are you Eileen?" the gentleman asked.

"Yes," I answered.

"William Blount," he said, stretching his hand out to me. "This is my daughter, Edwina," he added, nodding to the lady behind him.

126

Edwina Blount. That's what made the name sound familiar. I remembered a story Jack told me about her. So, this was the spoiled little rich girl that was responsible for Jack joining the service.

"Nice to meet the both of you," I said, shaking his hand and nodding to Edwina. "I hear you are renovating the Book. How can I help you?"

"I bought the hotel as an investment for Edwina. We would like to renovate the whole inside... new plumbing and lighting... new wallpaper... a completely new grand ballroom. We want to make it something very special," he said.

Edwina stood behind him, looking bored, and staring at the shelves of supplies. We indeed. She couldn't care less.

"Certainly, Mr. Blount," I said. "We have several catalogs behind the counter with samples of wallpaper, and lighting and plumbing fixtures. If the two of you don't see what you want, we can special order through several companies as well."

I had a feeling nothing from a catalog would do anyway.

"I'm sure you will find everything we sell to be top quality and our prices are very reasonable," I added.

The two of them thumbed through catalogs and discussed the samples when, suddenly, an idea came to me.

"Since you are taking everything down to renovate, have you considered insulating the place? I asked. "We can supply you with the very latest thing to hit the market, fiberglass insulation. It will pay for itself in no time."

"Fiberglass insulation... " Blount said, rubbing his chin. "Isn't that the stuff they developed for airplanes?"

"Yes sir, it is. You won't find anything better for the money."

"How's a pretty little thing like you know so much about these things?" Blount asked. "Is there a Mr. Eileen yet?"

"Not yet. But very soon. My Jack is off fighting in the war," I answered. Edwina snickered, then stopped short when she noticed me glaring at her.

"No offense, dear," Edwina meowed. "I'm sure your man is a good man. It just reminded me of a boy named Jack I once knew—a buffoon actually—I've heard he went in the war too."

"Ha!" Mr. Blount said. "You can say that again! "Why, I've never met such a useless young boy!" he said.

I could feel my blood boil. How dare this "Daddy Warbucks" and his spoiled little brat talk about Jack like that? I wanted to give both of them my two cents worth and more!

"You have yourself a new customer, young lady," Blount told me. "I will take the insulation too... nothing but the best for my little angel. I will send the contractors by first thing tomorrow to set up an account," he added. "I trust they can deal with you directly?"

Nothing but the best for her, my foot, I thought to myself. They wouldn't know a good man if they saw one! And she ain't no angel, I hate to tell ya. I was just about to give them a piece of my mind, when I saw Mr. Putnam standing toward the back of the store, smiling at me.

"Uh... yes, of course. Either myself or Mr. Putnam, the manager, would be happy to provide you with everything, right down to the last nail," I responded.

"Excellent. Good day!" Blount said, tipping his hat before the two of them strutted out of the store.

What a pair of despicable people! Actin' all holier than thou... they make me sick! I wasn't looking forward to dealing with them, and on a project the size of the Book, it would be for a long while too. The only satisfaction I would have is Pops, and possibly Jack, should the war keep going so well, taking some of their money from their cold, impersonal hands.

"You did good, Eileen," Putnam said, now standing beside me.

"Yeah, well you can deal with 'em from now on, Mr. P," I said.

"Good heavens! Why?" he asked.

"'Cause I don't wanna wind up bitin' my damn tongue off," I stated.

Across the street, the well-dressed mysterious man stood in the shadows of the recessed entryway of the five and dime, his large black Fedora pulled low over his face. He was looking at the young redhead talking to an older gentleman inside the lumber yard. He took a pencil sketch of a woman out of a manila envelope and held it up in front of him, comparing it to the girl inside the store. They looked remarkably similar.

CHAPTER TWENTY-TWO

A Friend in Need

November 29, 1944
Stalug Luft One
Barth, Germany

"Where's Leon?" I asked, bringing Mike into the barrack room. "This guy needs his help."

The others looked at Mike with looks of sorrow and pity; Kenny Paulsen, Walt Spindler, and a British officer that I hadn't seen before drew back when they smelled his burns.

"He went to the latrine... should be back soon," Robert said. "Isn't that the pilot that came in the other day?"

"Yeah. I didn't recognize him, but this is my friend Mike," I explained.

"Holy hell!" Joe Caparosa yelled. "Sit him down over here, by the stove."

"What the hell happened to you, Buddy?" Sidney asked Mike, looking at his badly burned face and hands.

The Brit, Paulsen, and Spindler retreated to the other side of the barracks, near Kenny's bunk and mumbled something I couldn't make out. The Brit held his nose and gave us a dirty look.

"He has a hard time talkin'," I told Sidney. "Who's Cap'n Limey over there?"

"I dunno his name," Sidney leaned in and told me. "I've seen him hangin' 'round with Walt and Kenny in the compound. Showed up here shortly after you stormed out. Those three are cookin' somethin' up... I think they're plannin' an escape," he added.

Leon came through the door carrying Lucky and noticed Mike sitting there.

"You got any of your remedies for this guy?" I asked him.

Leon walked over, put Lucky down and looked closely at Mike's wounds and winced.

"He's in pretty tough shape," Leon stated, "But his burns ain't as bad as they look. Let's get him lyin' down, and gimme a cool, wet cloth, would'ya?"

We led Mike to my bunk. I fumbled through my things and came up with a t-shirt and dipped it in a pot of water near the stove. Mike began to repeatedly sneeze and his eyes were watering.

"Poor guy. Now he's catching a cold too," Joe said.

Leon laid Mike back on the empty bunk, and placed the wet shirt over his face. Lucky climbed up on the bunk beside Mike and laid there purring.

"This should help soften his skin, so he can heal properly. It will also cool the burns," Leon explained.

Mike started sneezing almost non-stop. He sat up in the bunk and took the shirt off of his face. His eyes were puffy, red and watering. Tears streamed down his face. Leon carefully dabbed them dry.

"AHH-CHOOO!!" Mike sneezed loudly, sending Lucky streaking under Leon's bed.

"Goon up!!" Ray Prevost yelled. Everyone scattered about the room, preparing for inspection. I saw the Brit hide something in Kenny's bunk moments before Benny burst into the room.

"Goot Auf-ternoon," Benny said. "Who ees zhis man? Vhy ees he steel zitting down?" he asked, pointing at Mike.

"He's visiting," I said, helping him up off the bunk. Mike stood in front of the bunk and said nothing. Benny looked at him, before rifling through the bunk Mike had been sitting on.

"Vhat ees zhis??" Benny asked, holding up my wet t-shirt.

"It's a shirt," I deadpanned.

"I zee zat," Benny said, walking up to me, holding the shirt up. "Ees zhis yours?" He asked.

"Yeah," I answered.

"Ahh. Und tell me… vhy ees it vett? Washing zomezing? Getting rid auf zome dirt perhaps?" Benny questioned me.

"No," I said, offering no further explanation.

"I zeen you valking near barrack number zix earlier," Benny said. "That vas you, ya?"

I thought of where I'd been earlier. Barrack Six was along the fence facing the shoreline. It was the building I ducked behind to shake Mike. It was also a Brit barrack.

"Yeah. I was takin' a walk," I said. "Got a problem with that?"

"It's poshible," Benny answered. "May I zee your hands."

I held out my hands. Benny tossed the shirt back on the bunk and looked at my hands.

"Of course, You would not know anyzhing about zee hole in zee ground vee found under zhat barrack, vould you?" Benny asked, paying particular attention to my fingernails.

Out of the corner of my eye, I noticed the Brit, Kenny, and Walt putting their hands in their pockets.

"Not a damn thing," I answered.

"Auf course, you vouldn't," Benny said, continuing to search the rest of the room.

"I trust all auf you know zat digging holes ees strictly verboten!" Benny's voice echoed through the room while he searched every inch. "Do-ink so could earn zome time in zolitary…or vorse," he added, stopping in front of Kenny, Walt, and the Brit.

"Do you understand?" He asked.

"Yes, sir!" the three of them shouted, standing with their hands behind them, blocking Kenny's bunk. The look in their eyes suggested pure fear. I expected Benny would soon ask them to step aside, search the bunk, and the shit would hit the fan when he found what the Brit had hidden.

"Zhat ees goot!" Benny stated. He turned and looked over the entire room, before moving toward the door and opening it.

"Zhat ees all," he said, walking out and closing the door behind him.

That was close, I thought to myself. I don't know what the Brit had hidden in Kenny's bunk, but from their actions, I had little doubt that the three of them had something to do with the hole Benny was asking me about.

I sat back down on the bunk with Mike and noticed he had stopped sneezing and his eyes had stopped watering. Leon picked up my shirt and began to dab it on Mike's face again.

"We'll have to do this pretty often for it to work," Leon told me.

"Excuse me, how long is that man and this dreadful stench going to be here?" The Brit sneered.

"Long as he wants, or needs to be, pal," I said. "How long you gonna be here? Ain't you got someplace to be?" I added, making digging motions with my hands.

"Oh, very well," the Brit grumbled. "I trust I shall see the two of you this evening?" he asked Walt and Kenny. They both stared at the floor and shook their heads yes.

Good riddance, I thought, watching the Brit leave and shut the door behind him. I didn't know who he was, but I didn't like him. And now I had Benny suspecting me of whatever that damn Brit was planning. A lot of Brit airmen come from wealthy families. Because of that, I've noticed they tend to act snooty, and were only interested in their own well-being. This guy was definitely one of those. Likely, Walt and Kenny were doing his dirty work. I wondered what would have happened to them if Benny found what the Brit put in that bunk. I could sense him causing trouble.

"While you were gone, the Pow-Wow came," Joe said quietly. "It had good news too. The Allies took the town of Aachen. French troops made it through the Beffort Gap and reached the Rhine. They even took Strasbourg," he whispered to me.

"Don't forget about Rommel," Robert added.

"What about Rommel?" I asked.

"The bastard killed himself," Robert said quietly.

This was all good news. If the Allies could keep gaining ground, it would only be a matter of time before they started pushing to Berlin. A high ranking official killing himself was typically a good sign as well. I wished it could be Pickhardt next.

"I'm tellin' ya, We're gonna be outta this place by Christmas. I can just feel it," Sidney said.

"That's less than a month," Joe said. "I hope you're right, but I think that's a little optimistic."

I thought about getting out of here that soon. It would be a dream come true to be home with Eileen by then.

"You just wait an' see!" Sidney said, laying back on his bunk.

He took a drag off of his cigarette and began humming the song I'll Be Home For Christmas.

"Well, I'll be… " Leon said, looking at Mike's face.

"What?" I asked.

"I was noticing how soft his skin is where his eyes were watering," Leon said, looking at Mike's face.

Lucky jumped back up on the bunk and began to rub up against Leon.

"AHH-CHOOO!!" Mike sneezed. His eyes were red and watering again.

"It must be that damn cat of yours makin' him sneeze!" I shouted, swatting at Lucky to get him off the bunk.

Shortly after Lucky was gone, Mike's sneezing and watery eyes stopped.

"You may be right," Leon said, dabbing off Mike's face again. "Are you allergic to cats?" he asked Mike.

Mike shrugged his shoulders.

"I have an idea, if you're willing to try something," Leon told Mike. Mike shrugged and shook his head yes.

"Ain't nuthin' cleaner than your own tears, and they seem to help soften your burned skin. If a cat is makin' your eyes water, and we can capture and maintain that moisture, it may speed up your recovery," Leon said.

"You really think that will work?" Sidney asked.

"It might… long as you don't mind the symptoms," he said, looking at Mike. "All you'd have to do is hold Lucky on your lap now and then. Wanna give it a try?"

"S-s-s-ure… " Mike said. It seemed like a strange idea, but if it worked and eased Mike's pain, it would be worth it. Leon took a pack of cigarettes and a few chocolate bars from his Red Cross parcel, and stuffed them in his pockets.

"I'm gonna go see if I can trade for some bandages to hold that moisture in," he said.

"Okay," I said, dabbing Mike's face with my shirt.

"This guy seems to have some off-the-wall ideas that work," I reassured Mike. "Willie would have died and I could have lost a leg, if not for him."

Mike sat in silence, looking at me.

"G-g-ood to… s-s-see ya, S-s-shorty," he said.

"You too buddy!" I said, slapping him on the back. "Be nicer under different circumstances, but, you are a sight for sore eyes."

Mike chuckled and pointed at his eyes, more specifically, where his goggles had melted to his face.

"Sorry," I said. "Kind of a poor choice of words."

Mike patted me on the back and smiled. He still had his sense of humor, despite whatever hell he had been through. I knew he would eventually tell us about it, but for now, it was good to have someone here that I knew.

"Yep… I can see the Christmas lights of home already… " Sidney sighed.

"Shut up already," Joe said, lighting a cigarette and leaning back in his bunk. "You're gonna jinx our chances."

"No I'm not! I'll bet ya anything!" Sidney shot back, lighting his own cigarette, before settling back in his bunk again.

"Shhh! Listen!" Sidney whispered. The room went silent, and in the distance, I could make out the faint booming sounds. It sounded like bombs going off.

"I'll be hooome for Christmas… " he crooned.

CHAPTER TWENTY-THREE

The Beginning of the End

December 1, 1944
Stalug Luft One
Barth, Germany

A cold wind howled through the camp as we walked toward the north compound to get our potato rations for the week. I looked out over the Baltic as we walked along the fence line. A dull gray sky hung over the frozen water.

"So, what's the first thing you're gonna do, Joe?" Sidney asked.

"Huh?" Joe asked, looking puzzled.

"When ya get home, " Sidney replied. "It's December, ya know. We're gonna be goin' home soon."

"You still on that we'll be home by Christmas kick?" Joe grumbled.

"I'm tellin' ya, we're gonna be outta here soon; I can feel it in my bones!" Sidney exclaimed. "How 'bout you Jack?" he asked me.

"You gotta ask?" I said, pulling my collar up over my ears and stuffing my hands in my pockets. "I'm findin' my way to my gal. How 'bout you?"

"I meant after that," Sidney said. "Soon as I get back to Mt. Vernon, I'm goin' to the Whistle Stop diner on Broadway an' havin' the biggest steak they have in the place, and a big cold glass of milk straight from Wilson's dairy."

I thought of all the sights, sounds, and smells of back home. Strings of lights and popcorn on the Christmas tree, a warm home, a good meal, a comfortable bed… I could almost feel it all in my mind. I lit up a cigarette and found myself missing Eileen and everything back home in Detroit.

"Hadn't really thought about that," I said. "How 'bout you?" I asked Willie, who was walking along side of me.

"I'd just be happy to be home," Willie said. "What I'm doin' wouldn't matter."

"Kinda what I was thinkin'," I said.

"I can see myself fishin' in Rend Lake. Sittin' on the shore in the warm summer sun," Sidney said. "I'm tellin' ya I can already smell my hometown. Even the train car factory smells wonderful."

"That's exactly why I don't think about it til I know I'm goin' home," Joe said. "What happens when Christmas comes, and we're still here?" he asked. "I ain't settin' myself up to be disappointed again."

"Still nice to think about it," Sidney said.

As we walked past barrack number six, I noticed the Brit officer, Kenny, and Walt standing there talking to each other.

"Those two were out late last night," I said.

"I heard 'em come in just before it was time to go out for head count," Willie said. "They're cuttin' it pretty close."

" I don't like that damn Limey. He's gonna make trouble… I just know it," I said.

Willie shook his head yes. We all passed through the gate separating the south and north compounds.

"Just think—soon we won't have to haul potatoes—once we are home," Sidney said.

"You just ain't gonna stop, are ya?" Joe said.

"Nope. And I'll bet I'm right!" Sidney chimed.

"An' just what are ya gonna bet?!" Joe exclaimed. "You don't have anything."

"I'll kiss your ass in the middle of the compound on Christmas if we ain't out by then!" Sidney shouted.

"Wanna shake on that?" Joe said, holding out his hand.

Sidney shook his hand firmly. "It's a bet!" He told Joe.

"Good!" Joe said. "Now, button your damn lip about this home by Christmas shit!"

"Hey! Where's all the potatoes?" I said, noticing only a small pile where there was usually a huge wagon load.

"nur bloss erst funf Kartoffein!" the guard told us.

"What?!" Joe asked him. "Only five potatoes?! You're kiddin', right?"

The guard shrugged his shoulders. "Nur bloss erst funf Kartoffein," He said.

"I hope they have more of the other supplies," Sidney said.

"Nicht," the guard said, pointing at the small pile of potatoes. "nur bloss… "

"Yeah, yeah, we heard ya the first time!" Sidney shouted at him.

"Damn good thing the Red Cross sends us parcels, or we'd starve to death on what the Krauts give us," Joe solemnly said.

We silently gathered five potatoes each, and began to walk back to our barracks. I wondered why there was suddenly so few potatoes. That was usually something there was always a lot of. So much so, I was getting tired of them. It was the other things the Krauts gave us that were sparse.

"Damn it," Willie chuckled as we walked back along the fence line near the Baltic.

"What?" I asked.

"Now I can't get that big steak and glass of ice cold milk outta my mind," he answered.

I laughed. I had been picturing them in my mind too. We rounded the corner of Barrack Six and nearly ran into the Brit officer, who was standing beside the building. He jumped at the sudden sight of us. I noticed him quickly glance behind him, and toward the ground under the barrack.

"Have you seen Walt and Kenny?" Joe asked him.

"Why, I have no idea of their whereabouts," he replied coldly. His eyes were shifting all around the compound, to the nearby watchtower, and the ground. "Why?"

"There's a shortage of food," Joe told him. "If ya see 'em, let 'em know we need to discuss it."

The Brit shot him a surly look that suggested it was something he was not overly concerned about. I heard a stifled cough come from under the barrack. I moved closer and got right in the Brit's face.

"I dunno what you got cooked up, you Limey-ass pig, but I have my suspicions. You cause any trouble for them… " I said motioning my eyes to below the barrack. " …or any of us, an' I'll kick your snotty ass." I told him.

"Really," he said sarcastically.

"C'mon, Jack," Willie said. "Don't waste your time with him… or draw attention," he added, motioning to the ground.

"Have a nice day, Sergeant… " The Brit said, with added contempt for the word Sergeant as we walked away.

"Man, that guy pisses me off!" I grumbled.

"I know," Willie said. "We'll find a way to take care of him… just not at Walt and Kenny's expense."

He was right. I had little doubt they were under that barrack doin' the diggin' while that Limey watched. I had no doubt he planned it that way so he could walk away, leavin' them to get caught, if need be.

Entering our barrack, I noticed Mike sitting on my bunk with his face wrapped like a mummy, holding Lucky on his lap, all the while sniffling. Leon sat on his bunk reading a book. Ray Prevost was at the stove, pouring himself a cup of coffee.

"Pretty slim pickin's," Joe told him as we all put our potatoes in the bin. "They were only givin' us five of 'em this time," he added.

Normally, the bin would be heaped. It was only half full with what we put in, and likely wouldn't be full when the rest were added.

"They're shortin' us on bread too. One fifth a loaf per man a day," Ray said. "We're gonna be leanin' pretty hard on the parcels."

I walked over by Mike and looked at the ridiculous looking get-up.

"This workin'?" I asked Leon.

"I guess we'll see," he said. "It's time to take the bandages off."

Leon walked over to Mike, took Lucky off of his lap, sat him on the floor and began to unwrap Mikes face. When the bandages were removed, Mike's eyes were bloodshot and watering. His skin appeared pink and damp and much softer. The residue from his goggles that had been stuck to his face was nearly gone. The bandages were soaked and had dark stains from all that had been drawn out of Mike's skin.

"Looks a lot better," Leon said, dabbing a piece of clean cloth in a bowl of water and gently wiping Mike's face.

"I'll be damned. It does look better," I said. "Hows it feel, buddy?" I asked Mike.

He blinked his eyes and focused on me.

"A… lot… b-better," he said, feeling his own face. "It… feels… c-cooler." I noticed his speech was getting better as well.

"Good deal! Thanks, Leon," I said.

"Glad to see it works," Leon said. "We'll keep it up 'til we get all the crap out of his skin."

Mike made an attempt to smile, but the right side of his face was still pretty stiff.

"Appears you are in good hands," I told him. He sat silently and looked straight ahead, as if he was in deep thought.

"The l-last thing I r-rem-member was s-seein' the b-bastard c-comin' r-right at m-me… " Mike said. "a-and f-f-fire… " His eyes began to tear up. He shrugged his shoulders.

"It's okay, buddy. You're safe now," I reassured him.

" I-I- know. B-but, ehh-eh-ery t-time I c-close my e-eyes... "
he said, stopping short. He began to cry.

I knew exactly what he was talking about. I still relive my
crash every night. Getting used to it makes me wonder whether I'm
growing indifferent to the horrific deaths of my friends, just getting
a thicker skin, or if I'm losing my mind.

"It gets better over time, buddy," I lied.

The truth is, it doesn't, or it hasn't for me so far. It just gets
different. I went over to my bunk and got my journal. I sat on the
bunk across from Mike, opened it, and held it to him.

"I wrote this awhile back," I explained. " My plane was chopped
in half and I watched my whole crew go down. Some days it feels
like it was a few minutes ago; some days it feels like it was years ago,
but I still see 'em in my dreams. This doesn't stop the nightmares,
but it seems to help me get through the tough times."

Mike took the book and read the verse:

You know there is a saying
That sunshine follows rain.
And sure enough you'll realize,
That joy will follow pain.
Let courage be your password,
Make fortitude your guide.
And then instead of grousing,
Remember those who died.

The door burst open, and Benny and two other guards entered
the room.

"Zearch every einch!" Benny ordered them. All of us, with the
exception of Mike, stood silently and watched the guards search the

room high and low, overturning and moving everything in sight. Benny walked over to me, staring straight into my eyes.

"Goot mornink, Meester Glite," he said. I said nothing, but gave him a nod. I wondered what this Kraut imbecile was up to now.

"May I zee your hands please?" he asked.

"What for? Still think I'm up to something?" I asked.

"It's poshible," he replied, glancing at Mike, who was still sitting in my bunk.

I held my hands out in front of me. Benny looked closely at them, paying close attention to my fingernails again.

"Clean as a vhistle again... " Benny said.

He picked up the dirty, wet bandages that had been wrapped around Mike's face and looked at them.

"Und... you have vet, dirty towel een your bed, vunce again," he added.

"Hey! Them are bandages! And I had em wrapped around..." Leon started to say.

"Silence!" Benny yelled. "I am talkink to zhis man!"

Leon stopped talking.

"Care to explain zhis?" Benny asked, holding the bandages in front of me.

"I don't have to explain nothin', you crazy damn Kraut. I ain't done nothin'," I told him.

Benny looked at Mike, who sat dumfounded on my bunk.

"Get out auf zat bed!!" he ordered.

Mike got up and stood beside the bed. Benny grabbed the corner of the mattress and flung it on the floor and as he did, I heard the sound of something rolling around on the boards on the bottom of my bunk. I turned and saw a dirty powdered milk can laying there. It had tipped over and flung dirt all over the bottom of my bunk. Benny picked it up and held it in front of my face. He tipped it upside down, dumping the rest of the contents at my feet, while he stared into my eyes.

"Just as I zuspected," Benny said. "Und, I also zuzspect, you deed not deeg zat hole vee found under barrack seex by yourself," he added, shaking the can in my face.

"Zo tell me, Meester Glite… who else ees helpink you?"

"Go to hell," I told him.

"Guards!" Benny shouted, "Take zhis man away!" The two other guards grabbed me by the arms and carried me out of the barrack.

As they took me toward the North compound where the solitary confinement cells were, I become angrier by the minute. I knew damn well where that milk can came from, and who likely put it there, but wasn't about to rat out Walt and Kenny. I didn't know how, but I was gonna take care of that goddamn Brit when I got out, that was for sure.

When we went past Barrack Six, there stood none other than the Brit, talking to another German guard. He looked at me as the guards dragged me by. He smiled and waved at me.

"You sonofabitch!!" I screamed, trying to shake loose from the guards.

They grabbed onto me tightly, picked me up, and swiftly carried me away.

CHAPTER TWENTY-FOUR

The Stranger in Town

December 17,1944
Detroit, Michigan

The well-dressed stranger stood at the bus stop at the corner, staring at the lumber yard. Through the front windows, he saw the young red haired girl inside flip the sign in the front door from open to closed. He opened his ornate pocket watch and looked at the time. Five o'clock. She's right on time. When she turned to put her coat on, he stepped out onto the street and weaved his way through traffic, disappearing into the alley on the south side of the lumber yard.

"Good night Mister P," I said, locking the cash register.

"Good night Eileen," Mr Putnam said. "See you tomorrow! I'll get the door…"

I was looking forward to getting out of work. Tonight was the only night of the week I had all to myself; the first in many days. I opened the front and stepped outside and took a deep breath, breathing in the smell of the new snow that was falling. Mr Putnam locked the door behind me and waved goodbye.

I started walking north on Gratiot Avenue and hummed White Christmas to myself as the big white flakes fell slowly.

I love Christmas, and everything about it. It would be the best Christmas ever if I could spend it with Jack, but as each day ends, it looks like that isn't going to happen. My family and I listen to Armed Forces Radio every night to see how the war is going, and it seems to be going well for the Allied forces. Every day there is news about another victory, another town liberated, and German officials captured or killed. With each piece of good news, the chances of Jack coming home soon are getting better.

I stopped for the cross walk and wondered how he was doing. When the signal light changed, I looked both ways before crossing, and out of the corner of my eye, I noticed that strange man walking up behind me. When I turned to look at him, he ducked into Hudson's store.

Who is that guy? Why do I keep seeing him around? I kept walking and as the snow began to fall heavier, I thought about Jack again. I hoped to hear from him soon. His letters are a not only reassurance for me that he is okay, they make him seem closer. They are also a welcome break from my daily routine, and dealing with the Blounts, who are getting under my skin more each day.

I heard footsteps behind me. They seemed to be picking up the pace and getting closer. I glanced over my shoulder and saw the stranger approaching again. Is he following me? I began to walk a little faster. The sound of an engine racing and brakes screeching echoed out of the alley behind me.

"Hey, Red!" I heard an unmistakable voice shout.

I turned around to see Pop's truck parked across the middle of the sidewalk, and the stranger standing on the other side. His right hand was in his coat pocket and he had a surprised look on his face.

"What'cha lookin' at, Bub?" Pops asked him, opening his door to reveal the shotgun hidden beside the seat.

The stranger looked at the gun and the two burly workers Pops had hired who were getting out of the passenger's side.

"If ya know what's good for ya, you'll take a walk… NOW," he added.

The stranger loosened his grip on the cold metal object in his pocket, turned around and began to walk away.

"Need a lift, Red?" Pops asked me.

146

"Sure Pops… you have room?" I answered.

"I'll always have room for you, Red," Pops said. "This here is my workers, Elmer and Fred. Guys- this is my soon-to-be daughter, and the apple of my eye, Eileen," He said.

I looked up at the two muscular men in front of me with their hats clenched in their hands.

"Hello," I said and smiled.

"Ma'am," they both replied and nodded.

"Eileen is who got me the job at the Book… and who you have to thank for your jobs," Pops told them.

"Much obliged, Ma'am," they said before crawling into the back of the truck.

"You're welcome!" I said, getting into the passengers side and closing the door. "And I prefer you just call me Eileen… Ma'am is what people call my mom."

"Okay, Miss Eileen," they answered.

"Speakin' of the Book," I said to Pops, "How's the job goin'?"

"Finer than frog hair, Red," Pops said. "I got two good workers and a lot of steady work."

"And the Blounts?" I asked as we drove away.

"They're somethin' else," Pops chuckled. "The old man's got more money'n brains, and that girl of his… she musta been born with assholes for eyes."

"Why do you say that?" I laughed, giving him an odd look.

"'Cause she's got a shitty outlook on everything! Oops… sorry 'bout the language, Red," He said.

"No need to apologize. I couldn't have put it better myself," I told him. "Some days, I could just grab her by the throat and… "

"Don't let 'em get to ya, Red," Pops warned. "Folks like that just plain ain't happy, no matter what. Maybe it's havin' all that money that does it to 'em."

He tapped me on the shoulder. "Guess we'll never know 'bout

that!" he said, letting out a hearty laugh.

"Hey! What happened to this goldmine you promised me?!" I asked. Pop's laugh echoed through the truck.

"We're workin' on that, Red," He chuckled, pulling up to the curb in front of our house. "Jus' promise ya won't turn into Edwina when ya get it, okay?

"That's a promise I know I can keep!" I exclaimed, getting out of the truck. "Thanks for the ride Pops." I said.

"No problem, Red," he said. I began to walk to the house and stopped.

"Hey Pops… " I said, turning around, thinking of the stranger that was following me.

"Yeah?" he answered.

" Did you see…" I didn't know how to put it.

"Don't you worry 'bout him," Pops said as Elmer and Fred got back in the front seat, "I got my eye on him."

"Okay," I responded.

I walked to the house, found the mailbox empty and went through the front door. My dad was sitting in his easy chair, smoking a cigar and listening to The Adventures of Ozzie and Harriet on the radio. My sisters were all gathered on the floor in front of it.

"Welcome home, dear!" my mom said. "Looking for this?" she asked holding up a tri-fold postcard from Jack. My eyes lit up.

"Yes!!" I shouted, grabbing the note from my mom.

"Supper is almost done, dear. We're having your favorite!" she said, returning to the kitchen. "And I made some rice pudding for dessert!" echoed from the kitchen.

I took my coat off and curled up in my mom's chair and opened it and began to read:

Hows my Honey? Still love me? Sure you're not lyin'?
I'm still here and doing fine, but I can't wait until

I can come home and hold you in my arms. I was hoping it would be for Christmas, and a couple of the guys have a bet running regarding that.

I have some other news. Do you remember Mike? He is here in the same camp as me! Small world, huh? He came in awhile ago, and has some burns, but is in the good care of another friend here.

It's nice having someone I know here to pass the time with.

Don't worry about me sweetheart, I am safe here. About the only thing I could die from is boredom. Or missing my Honey. I can't wait to get home and see you and everyone again. If I'm not back by then, I wish you a Merry Christmas. If not, we'll have many more of them when we start our life together.

Your Jack, XOXOXOXOXO

P.S. Tell your mom, dad and "the kids" I said hi!

I folded the note back up and held it against me. I remembered meeting Mike when he came here with Jack one time when they were on leave. He seemed like a wonderful fellow. I'm glad he and Jack wound up in the same place, but wished it were under different circumstances. I wish I knew what it was like there. I'd give anything to see Jack for Christmas.

"And now, here is the latest news from Armed Forces Radio!" the radio announcer said.

I settled in near the radio and listened carefully. My mom walked into the living room to listen as well.

"The country of Greece has fallen into civil war and has seen many clashes between the Democratic

Army of Greece, backed by the U.S. and Great Britain, and the Greek Communist Party, aided by troops from Bulgaria, Yugoslavia, and Albania. The city of Athens has now been placed under martial law.

In the Ardennes region of Belgium, the Germans have launched an offensive against Allied Forces in what is being called the Battle of the Bulge along the Belgian, French and Luxumbourg borders. The Germans used 1600 artillery pieces and shelled the Allies in an eighty mile stretch of the front for over ninety minutes. Heavy casualties are being reported. A heavy snowstorm in the area has kept Allied aircraft grounded, but it has also slowed the Germans advance. According to reports, many German tank and artillery units are bogged down in the heavy snow.

This just in: sources have reported that Wassen SS Forces have killed eighty-one unarmed American prisoners of war near the town of Malmedy in Belgium."

"Oh dear," my mom said. "Is that anywhere near Jack?" she asked.

"I don't think so," I said, looking at the address on his post card to double check. "He is in Barth, Germany."

"That was in Belgium, my dear," my dad told her. "It must have been a part of this latest offensive. The S.S. must have killed them on the spot."

"Dad, What's an S.S.?" Dot asked.

"From what I've read, they are very loyal to Hitler, and very violent as well," he answered her. "Just be glad Jack hasn't had to deal with them. Speakin' of, how is he doing?" my dad asked.

"He says he is doing well, but misses home and all of you. It must be safe where he is. He says he is bored. He also wishes everyone a Merry Christmas," I told them. "Do you remember Mike? The fellow he brought here once?"

"Yes," my mom said.

"He is in the same camp as Jack now. He came in awhile back." I said.

"Oh my!" My mom said. "At least there is someone he knows there now."

"Yeah," I said.

The news of prisoners of war being killed worried me. What if that becomes a trend now that the Germans are losing ground in the war? I read and re-read his postcards that tell me all is well and he is safe, but I also feel he doesn't tell me everything that is going on there. It would be his nature to keep me from worrying.

I closed my eyes and thought of Jack, trying to picture him and what he was going through. Please be safe, and know that I love you, I thought to myself. And stay away from the S.S... whatever that is.

CHAPTER TWENTY-FIVE

I'm So Happy, I Can't Stop Cryin'

December 16, 1944
Stalug Luft One
Barth, Germany

Time, or even life for that matter, has a way of blurring while in solitary that I can't describe. There are no days. There are no nights either. It's just time, and the minutes go by like hours. Sleep is the only reprieve, but being here makes my nightmares worse, and much more graphic. Awakening from a nightmare to total darkness is almost a nightmare in itself. That darkness is absolute at times, and I live for whatever light can shine in the small slit on the side of the cell.

Seeing light is the only means of keeping track of days. Keeping track of the days is the only means of knowing how much longer I'll be in here. By international law, they're not supposed to keep anyone in solitary more than twenty days. It doesn't always work out that way, but it gives something to look forward to.

There is also silence. Not a brief spurt where, by chance, everything quiets down at the same time, it's complete silence. For hours. At times, it can be deafening.

I've been sitting here for a while watching light from the rising sun pierce through the slit in the wall behind me and illuminate a small area of the wall in front of me.

I can make out two sections of five marks, and four more lines scratched on the wall. I picked up a small piece of limestone from the floor and scratched a line through the four, marking fifteen days. I stared at the marks and wondered if I could do another five days. One day at a time, I murmured to myself. I have to think small like that. I would drive myself insane otherwise. I looked away from my marking and at the many things others before me had scratched in the wall. Just above my marking, I noticed something written on the wall. I wiped the dust off of it and began to read,

> I'm sitting here thinking of all the
> things I left behind.
> It's hard to put down what's running
> through my mind.
> I've flown in a batch of airplanes,
> over a hell of a batch of ground.
> A drearier place this side of hell is
> still waiting to be found.
> But there is one consolation,
> sit closer while I tell.
> When I die, I'll go to Heaven,
> for I've done my hitch in Hell.

Amen to that, I said, leaning back against the wall. I thought of back home and Eileen for the hundredth time since I'd been here. It sure looked as if I wouldn't be home for Christmas. But then again, being stuck in here, I had no idea what was going on with the war. Things were going well for the Allies when I went in. Hopefully, they still were.

My blood began to boil thinking about how that lousy Brit got me tossed in here. If it's the last thing I do, I'm gonna make sure he gets what is coming to him. I knew he would be trouble. I just didn't think it would wind up to be for me.

I'd like to get that numbskull Benny alone for a few minutes too. I didn't do a damn thing to deserve this.

I heard the sound of footsteps approaching. Most likely it was time for the bread and water I get once a day. I watched for the small opening at the bottom of the door to open, so the food could be shoved in, but heard the sound of the lock turning instead. Am I being released? The door opened and bright light filled the cell. When I was able to focus my eyes, I noticed Benny and the two other guards standing outside the cell.

"Goot mornink, Meester Glite," he said. I stared at him for awhile.

"It will be if you're lettin' me outta this hell hole," I said.

"Ya," he said. "You have zome very goot friends, Meester Glite. Zhey have been speakink very well on your behalf," he added.

"What the hell are you talkin' about?" I asked.

"Your roommates," Benny explained. "Zhey have been vurking hard to get you… how you say… released. You are free to go back to your barrack now."

I couldn't believe my ears. I'm free?? I jumped up, walked out of the cell and into the bright light outside. I took a deep breath of fresh air and let it out. Free.

"Zhey vill take you back," Benny said, pointing at the two guards. "Und I vill be vatchink you very closely."

"You do that, Benny," I told him. "I still ain't got nothin' to hide."

Walking back to the barrack, I noticed how weak and wobbly I felt. I needed some food to build my strength back up. As horrible as the straw filled mattresses in our bunks are, mine is going to feel like a cloud compared to the wooden bench in solitary.

I couldn't wait to get back and hear what has been going on with the war and with Leon's makeshift treatments for Mike.

"Hey! Look who's back!" Sidney shouted as I came through the door.

Ray and Roscoe were sitting at the table, playing cards. They both looked up and gave me a nod and a smile.

"Good to see ya, Jack," Willie said, shaking my hand and patting me on the back.

"Welcome back!" Leon and Joe yelled.

"Thanks!" I said. "It's good to be outta that place. Word is you guys did some tall talkin' to get me out?" I asked.

"Yeah. We all gave 'em our two cents worth," Joe told me. "But it was your pal there that chewed their ears off," he said, pointing to the other side of the room.

Mike was sitting on the bunk next to mine, smiling at me. His burns still looked terrible, but his face was now a light pinkish color.

"Hey Shorty! Long time, no see!" he said. He could move his lips freely and his speech was almost back to normal.

"Damn! You're doin' a lot better!" I said.

"Yes, I am," He said. "Leon's idea worked like a charm."

"That's good! And thank you all for gettin' me out!" I said, noticing Walt and Kenny weren't in the room.

"So, fill me in. What's been goin' on? Any breaking news from the front?" I asked.

"We're hearing a lot of bombing at night," Joe told me. "Word has it the Krauts started a big attack in Belgium in the Ardennes region too. Heavy snowstorms have kept our planes grounded, so they made up some good ground. Only good thing is, the Kraut's tanks and artillery are gettin' stuck in the snow though. The whole thing looks like it could be a long hard battle."

"And around here?" I asked. "Walt and Kenny still hanging around with Cap'n Limey?"

The room went silent and everyone had somber looks on their faces.

"Coupla days after you got tossed in the clink, they finished that tunnel," Sidney said.

"They got out?" I asked.

"Naw. They made it outside the fence line... but not much farther. Both of 'em was gunned down," Sidney told me.

I couldn't believe what I was hearing. Planning and attempting an escape is a dangerous thing to do. Much like flying a bombing mission, it requires a lot of teamwork and absolute trust in your team. The kind of trust where you can place your life in someone else's hands knowing they will protect it, no matter what. My crew and I had that trust. I didn't see that with the Brit officer.

"What about that damn Brit?" I asked.

"He somehow made it back to his barracks," Joe said. "Krauts found him and all the others sleepin' like babies."

"That son of a bitch," I said. "He not only used 'em to do the dirty work, he used 'em as shields too?"

All of them shook their heads yes. I couldn't help but wonder if Walt and Kenny would be alive today, had I ratted them out to Benny.

"We need to teach the bastard a lesson," I said.

"We're workin' on that," Joe said, giving me a evil grin.

I didn't know what they had planned for him, but I wanted to be a part of it. The wheels in my own head were spinnin' as well, trying to think of a way to make his life hell. My stomach let out a long, rumbling growl that sounded like a distant thunderstorm.

"Anything cookin' Roscoe? I'm 'bout starved to death," I asked.

"Not yet. Waitin' to see what we get—or if we get," he answered.

I noticed the potato bin was empty. I didn't see any other vegetables or rations either.

"Still shortin' us?" I asked.

"Yeah. It's worse than ever. We've had to resort to eatin' in the mess. And all they have is barley soup that gets clearer every day. Nuther coupla days an' it'll just be dirty water," Sidney told me.

"Did I get any Red Cross parcels?" I asked.

"Not while you were in the clink," Sidney told me. "An' what we got was shorted a lot of stuff. We're hopin' to get some rations and parcels today, otherwise we'll just have to go hungry."

"Any mail?" I asked.

"We ain't had mail in over a week," Joe told me. "We've heard the Allies took out the train tracks."

I sat on my bunk and lit a cigarette. When I went into solitary, there was nothing but good news. The Allies were winning one battle after another. Joe and Sidney were arguing whether or not we'd all be home for Christmas. Although I thought Sidney's prediction was a long shot, I figured if not then, it wouldn't be long after.

Now there is news of a new German offensive that is going well for them so far. It looks and feels like we'll be here awhile with both sides bogged down fighting a hard fight in bad weather.

Ever since I've been here, food could always be found. Whether it'd be something you wanted was debatable, but it was there. Now, food is getting scarce. The parcels we depend on are being shorted and we don't know when our next meal will come.

On top of all that, two of my roommates are dead, and I can't help but feel partly to blame.

I laid back on my bunk and watched the smoke from my cigarette trail upward.

It's strange how fast things can go to hell in a hand basket around here.

CHAPTER TWENTY-SIX

All I Want for Christmas

December 21, 1944
Detroit, Michigan

"I'll be hooome for Christmas… you can count on me…" I sang along to the radio while I poked a needle through a kernel of popcorn. I stopped to wipe a tear from my eye.

"How's that?" my dad asked from under the Christmas tree.

"A little to the left, dear," my mom told him. "There! Oh… no… back to the right… just a bit."

"Please have snow… and mistletoe… " I sang. My voice cracked a bit toward the end.

"And presents on the tree!!" my sisters sang in harmony.

This song makes me think of Jack every time I hear it. I so wanted him home for Christmas. At one time it looked possible, but the news about German success in the Battle of the Bulge seems to have turned the tides for now. It appears the war will rage on for who knows how long.

"Look at how long mine is!" Rosie shouted, standing on her tiptoes holding a string of popcorn up. There was still another foot of stringed corn on the floor.

"Wow!" Doe exclaimed. "Look at mine!" she said holding hers up to show an even longer strand.

"Oh dear," my mom said. "Now it's leaning forward. Tip it back a bit dear, so it doesn't fall."

"Oh, good night, nurse!" Dad's voice echoed from inside the tree. "How's that?"

"Perfect!" my mom shouted.

As I poked the needle through several kernels of corn and pushed them down the thread, I wondered why Jack hadn't written in a while. His notes had become quite regular since he got to prison camp. I couldn't help but think about the news of prisoners of war being killed. How horrible that must have been. He's alright, I told myself. It is a busy time of year for mail.

"Christmas Eve will find me… where the love light gleams…" I sang.

"Hear you are, dear," I heard my mom say.

She was standing in front of me, holding the golden star for the top of the tree. "I think you should put this on… and don't forget to make a wish," she told me.

"Okay," I said, taking the star from her.

"Be careful, Dollface," my dad said, holding the ladder for me. I climbed the ladder and placed the star on the top of the tree and looked at it. I planted a kiss on the palm of my hand and blew it toward the star. A sad smile came across my face.

"I'll be hoooome for Christmas… If only in… my dreams…" I sang, looking at the star through my tears.

from POW journal

CHAPTER TWENTY-SEVEN

A Bet is a Bet, Buddy

December 25, 1944
Stalug Luft One
Barth, Germany

"That's pretty damn good." Mike told me, looking over my shoulder at the picture of Eileen I had just drawn in my journal.

"Thanks," I replied. "It makes her seem closer."

Mike sat down next to me at the table and studied the drawing.

"Hell, this makes me miss her too. You're a lucky man, Shorty," He said.

"I suppose I am," I said. "But I'd feel luckier if I was home."

"I know what ya mean. Merry Christmas, my friend," he said, patting me on the back.

"Same to you," I replied.

"Merry Christmas, Sidney," Joe said loudly. "Emphasis on the word Christmas... what was that you was sayin' 'bout Christmas a while back? Believe we had a bet?"

"Go ahead. Rub it in," Sidney replied. "But I'll bet I'm not far off..."

"Don't go makin' bets til ya pay off the one ya already made!" Joe chuckled. "Lemme see... what was that bet again?"

Leon, Ray, and Robert entered the room, shaking off the cold. They sat at the table and Robert signaled for everyone to gather around. We all gathered silently around the table, looking at Robert.

"We just read the latest Pow-Wow. There was good news for a change," he said quietly. "The snow storms that kept Allied aircraft grounded at the Bulge have cleared. They are bombing the hell out of the Krauts as we speak."

"See? I told ya I wasn't far off!" Sidney proclaimed.

"Any good news regarding our rations?" Joe asked.

"Word has it we've been gettin' shorted so they can send it to the troops at the front fightin' the Bulge. I guess if we win there, we'll start gettin' it back," Robert answered.

"I sure hope so," Sidney said.

"We best be gettin' out to head count. It's almost 2000 hours," Willie said.

"Hey! Didja hear? The guy over in the north compound finished that violin!" Joe announced as we filed outside. "The Krauts are even gonna let him play it for us, bein' Christmas an' all."

The harsh reality of missing Christmas at home began to set in as we began to stand in rows and wait to be counted. I didn't think it was possible to miss Eileen any more than I did right now. I knew this was her favorite time of year, and, with no mail service, I hadn't been able to send a note. I hoped she was doing well, and her Christmas would be good.

"There's Violin Guy," Willie leaned in and told me.

I wasn't expecting much from a violin made in a prison camp. I was expecting a box with a neck and God knows what for strings, but I was impressed. It looked just like a real store-bought violin. As he took his place among the lines of hundreds of prisoners, the guards began to appear to do the count.

"About that bet..." Joe said, elbowing Sidney. Sidney stared straight ahead with his cigarette in the corner of his mouth.

"What about it?" Sidney asked.

"You a man of your word, or what?" Joe asked him. Sidney stomped out his cigarette and let out a long sigh.

"After you," he asked Joe.

"Oh no, after you... I insist!" Joe responded, extending his arm to the center of the compound.

The two of them walked into the center of the compound without saying a word. Some German guards noticed them leaving their places in line.

"Halt! Weider!" they shouted walking toward Joe and Sidney.

Joe undid his belt, unbuttoned his pants and let them fall to the ground. The guards stopped and watched as Sidney knelt on the ground behind Joe, grabbed him by the thighs and planted a long kiss on his ass.

The whole camp erupted in laughter as Joe calmly pulled his pants back up, re-buttoned them, and buckled his belt. The pair turned precisely and marched back, turned with precision, and took their places in line.

The guards looked bewildered at each other, shrugged their shoulders and went back to counting.

"You two have gone insane, ya know that?" Ray told them.

"A bet is a bet…" Joe said.

"And nobody can say I ain't a man of my word…" Sidney added.

When the laughter began to subside, I heard the sound of the violin playing "Silent Night." The violin sounded wonderful. This was no toy violin; it sounded as nice as any I've heard. One by one, prisoners began to sing the lyrics, until every man was singing loudly.

"Silent Night! Holy Night! All is calm… all is bright!"

Behind us, I heard someone singing in German, "Stille Nacht… Heilige Nacht… alles schlaft… Einsam Wacht…"

I turned and saw Benny standing there singing loudly. We looked directly at each other, and between verses, he smiled at me. I smiled back.

When the song ended we began to walk back to the barracks for lights out.

"Merry Chreezmas, my friend," Benny said when I walked past him. I was shocked. Benny and I have had a mutual hate and distrust since I got here, yet he was wishing me a Merry Christmas.

"Merry Christmas, Benny," I said, wondering if tomorrow it'd be back to business as usual between us.

I walked into my barracks, pulled my Red Cross parcel from under my bed out and sat it next to me. My stomach let out a long, low rumble as I looked through the contents. I took the last biscuit and four raisins from it and chewed them slowly. Hopefully, it would be enough to stave off my hunger pangs long enough to get some sleep. When I finished, I lit a cigarette and stretched out in my bunk just as the power and lights went out. I thought of Eileen and her family and the feast they were likely enjoying. Dad and Aunt Margaret would be doing the same. Man, I wish I could be there.

I took a long drag and listened to the sounds of bombs going off in the distance. Definitely NOT a silent night for some.

"Hey guys!" Sidney whispered. "Come lookit this!" he added, pointing out the window.

We all crowded at the window and looked out. Along with the sounds of the bombs we could see bright flashes of light. During the brief flashes of light I could see plumes of heavy smoke in the distance. I could make out the sound of airplanes.

"They ain't never been that close," Willie said.

"Come get us, boys. We're waitin'…" Robert said.

CHAPTER TWENTY-EIGHT

My Stomach Thinks My Throat's Been Cut

January 9, 1945
Stalug Luft One
Barth, Germany

Jerry Rations

Of our food we get in "Kriegieland"
what little there is of it
Some was not quite what we eat at home
but we learn to love it.
With Red Cross food gone "Kapoot"
due to snafu-ed transportation
there was nothing left for us to do
but depend on "Jerry Rations"
I've got them all, if I recall
There's nothing I have missed
So let's take each item one by one,
and go right down the list."

I stopped and read what I had just written in my journal. Under it, I made two columns, then drew a small potato with a halo around it in the upper left.

"What 'cha doin'?" Mike asked.

"Listin' all the stuff we got to eat… and comin' up with descriptions that rhyme," I said. I wrote POTATOES, the glorious spud beside the picture.

I scribbled down a verse next to the potato and read it aloud,

"This nourishing stuff was the Jerries' best bet—mashed, boiled, or fried—we ate all we could get."

"I like that!" Mike chuckled. "What 'cha got next?" he asked.

In the upper right column, I drew a steaming bowl with the word SOUP next to it.

"Lemme do one for that!" Mike exclaimed. I handed him my journal.

As he wrote he muttered, "They gave us soup in quite a variety, few of which we'd eat, back in society!"

"What the hell are you guys doin'?" Robert asked, waking from a nap.

"It's a list of things the Krauts give us," I told him. "Just tryin' to pass the time. We are comin' up with rhymes for everything… wanna try it?" I asked.

"Why not?" Robert said. "What do you have so far?" he asked.

"Potatoes and soup," Mike answered.

Robert sat up and looked at our supply bins.

"How 'bout that awful stuff?" he said, pointing at the small amount of colaraba we had.

"Okay," I said, drawing a picture of a colaraba under the potato in the left column. "What do you want to say about it?"

Robert thought for a minute and said "Here's the colla-robby, the worst veg' they had, but when a man's hungry, it isn't half bad."

"Ain't that the truth!" Leon chuckled, pouring himself a cup of coffee from the pot on the stove.

I drew a picture of a coffee pot under the soup bowl.

"Your turn!" I told Leon. "Gimme something about that coffee."

Leon took a swig of his coffee, grimaced, and thought about it.

"The coffee they gave us was known as ersatz, but with the Red Cross stuff gone, it is really the cat's ass," he replied.

We all laughed out loud.

"Listen!" Willie shouted. The room fell silent. Outside in the distance we could hear bombs going off, and the unmistakable sound of a squadron of airplanes. They sounded closer then they did yesterday.

"Come on, guys! Keep them bombs droppin'!" Mike said.

"How 'bout you Willie?" I asked "Wanna add something to this?"

"Yeah. Carrots," he answered.

I drew a picture of a carrot in the left column, under the colaraba.

"And your rhyme?" I questioned him.

"We didn't like 'em as G.I.'s, but it was kinda funny. As Kriegies we ate almost as much as Bugs Bunny," he said.

"Sure would be nice if we actually had some food instead of sittin' here writin' about it," Mike sighed.

"No kiddin'," Sidney commented.

The air raid sirens suddenly began to wail.

"Where's Joe and Roscoe??" Sidney asked.

All of us had to be in our barracks as soon as the sirens sounded.

"They are seein' if they can get some rations!" Mike shouted over the siren.

Just then, Joe and Roscoe both burst into the room, slamming the door behind them. Joe set a loaf of bread on the table and Roscoe carried what appeared to be a piece of meat wrapped in paper to the table next to the stove.

"Did ya hear the bombs and planes?" Joe asked over the piercing din of the siren.

"We could SEE them, they were so close!" Roscoe yelled, joining us around the table.

My stomach let out a growl that could almost be heard over the siren. I realized I hadn't eaten anything in nearly two days. The air raid sirens began to wind down to a stop.

"What 'cha got over there?" I asked, pointing to the meat on the table.

"Appears to be horse meat," Roscoe answered. "Looks like we'll get something in our bellies today anyway," he added, unwrapping the chunk of meat the size of a powdered milk can.

"What are youse doin' here?" Joe asked, looking at my open journal.

"Passin' the time by comin' up with things about the food here," I answered.

"Lemme see…" Joe said.

I slid the book to him and he read while he sawed off a thin slice of bread.

"I got one for this damn bread," he said.

I took the journal back and drew a loaf of bread.

"Go ahead…" I told him.

"This Jerry version of the staff of life was made of such stuff it defied even a knife!" he responded, taking the lid off of the margarine and spreading a thin layer on his slice of bread.

I drew a picture of the margarine can and thought about the taste.

"How 'bout as for the marge', we ate it and muttered, this is, at best, a poor substitute for butter?" I asked.

"Amen to that!" Sidney chuckled, slicing off his own thin slice of bread.

"While we was out, we got a chance to look at the latest edition of the Pow-Wow," Joe said quietly. "The Krauts are pullin' out of the Ardennes. Looks like The Battle of the Bulge is over," he added.

"That's good!" Sidney said. "I need to get outta this place. My damn stomach thinks my throat's been cut."

Supplies have been very sparse since Christmas. We have resorted to eating whatever we can get our hands on and eating it slowly to fool our stomachs. Lately my stomach has been getting wise to that.

"All I got is cabbage, a small piece of colaraba, and this meat," Roscoe explained while he seasoned the meat, "It'll go a lot farther if we make a soup," he told us.

"Soup it is then," Robert sighed. We all shook our heads in agreement. I drew a picture of a head of cabbage in the journal and thought of the nasty tasting saurkraut the Krauts had been giving us. It was nearly black and we could barely get it down.

While I watched Roscoe chop the head of cabbage up and put it into the large pot on the stove, I wrote; "The cabbage received a new high priority, and was relished in soup by a great majority."

"Got one for the meat we get yet?" Sidney asked me.

"Not yet," I answered, smelling the pungent odor of the horse meat Roscoe was cutting up for the soup. "Any suggestions?" I asked, drawing a picture of canned meat and a likeness of a chunk of fresh meat tied in string that we occasionally get.

"They gave us meat in a roll or a can. If you could hold it down, you was a damn good man," Sidney said.

I thought about eating horse meat, and wondered if I would keep it down. I had heard that some barracks had resorted to eating rats. I'm wasn't that desperate yet.

"Wonder how Sir Reginald likes his new digs?" Willie asked.

"Who?" I asked. It was a name I'd never heard before.

"Lt. Col. Reginald Archibald, III," Willie explained. "Believe you know him as Cap'n Limey."

He had fallen off of my "get even" radar when getting food became a priority. I realized I hadn't seen him the past couple of days.

"What about him?" I asked.

A sly smile came across the faces of Joe, Robert, and Willie.

"I overheard that someone had completed a tunnel out of this place," Joe leaned in and whispered.

"Did that bastard get out?!" I fumed.

Joe shook his head no. "When I overheard that a tunnel had been completed, I may, or may not, have let the information slip while Robert and I just happened to be walkin' past Barrack Six."

"Where's this tunnel at? How come I never heard a damn thing about it?" I whispered.

"I never seen it myself. I just heard it was under Barrack Four. Ya know, the north side. The one that faces the Baltic. It is pretty much out of sight and very dark at night," Joe answered.

I could picture the area in my mind. It would be a good place to try and dig out. The spotlights are blocked by buildings, and here of late, there haven't been as many foot patrols.

"I might have casually mentioned what I had heard about it to Benny," Willie said, smiling at Joe and Robert. "He did thank me and tell me he would see to it my barrack would get something for my co-HOP-eration. What was it again? Oh yeah! Some meat," he added.

I looked at Roscoe adding the last of the meat to the pot and smiling at me.

"Yeah but, what's that gotta do with... Sir,,, whatever his name is?" I asked.

"There was no tunnel, there was just a hole about four feet deep, but Sir Reginald didn't know that," Robert explained. "Benny and two other guards caught him red-handed tryin' to crawl under barrack four the night before last."

A smile came across my face.

"Zee puneeshment for beink caught een zee auct auf escapink is vewy, vewy severe!" Joe said, mocking Benny's poor English. "He got tossed in the clink for the maximum," he added.

"I'll be damned!" I said. "Wait a minute! Why wasn't I involved in this?" I asked.

"With Benny watchin' your every move?" Willie asked. "It was best you didn't know a damn thing about it."

I chuckled to myself thinking about the elaborate scheme they had come up to with get even with the Brit. So, Cap'n Limey got tossed in solitary. Good for him. He deserved that, and a lot more.

The air raid sirens began to wail again. I could hear the voices of people scurrying about outside our barrack. Over the sirens I could hear an occasional bomb. They must be close if I could hear 'em over the racket the sirens were making. I sat back and lit a cigarette and listened for more bombs and planes in the distance.

The Battle of the Bulge was drawing to a close, and looked to be yet another Allied victory. Going home might not be so far off now. I took a long drag and exhaled.

The air raid sirens began to wind down again and I could hear the bombers quite clearly. We crowded the windows and looked out to see squadrons of B-17's dotting the sky line to the south. I took a puff off of my cigarette and listened to that wonderful sound of radial engines fade away as the planes disappeared over the horizon.

When they were gone, I started having flashbacks of going down in the Purple Heart. Beads of sweat covered my brow as I walked away from the window.

I thought about my crew and wondered if more survived. I wondered where Ortlip had been taken to and if he was doing alright. It'd been a little over three months since the Purple Heart had gone down, but some days it felt like it was yesterday.

Three months would have been enough time to be pretty close to finishing our twenty-five, and thinking about going home. I took another drag and let out a heavy sigh with my exhale. My stomach let out a long, reverberating, slow growl. The soup Roscoe was cooking would be the first real meal of sorts we'd had in weeks.

I walked back to the table, picked up my pencil and began to write in my journal.

There it is, that's all the food,
that Jerry ever rationed.
At any rate, that's all I got
at the Stalug where I was stationed.
I hope our Air Force takes it easy
on Red Cross 'transportations'
that we may have something to eat
besides these 'Jerry Rations'.

"Hey guys…" I said as I re-read all the things we had come up with. They all stopped what they were doing and looked at me.

"Yeah?" Mike asked me.

"I've noticed something in all of these descriptions," I said. "They are all in past tense."

"What do you mean?" Joe asked.

"Look at 'em…" I replied, turning the book around for all to see. "I see a lot of 'they gave us', or 'it was', not give us, or it is. Like we were looking back at it. That supposed to be a sign?" I asked.

"It could be," Sidney pondered. "Maybe in the back of our minds we feel we'll be soon gettin' outta this joint?" he asked.

"Or that we want to," Willie added.

We all sat silently and thought about it.

"Beats the alternative," Robert said. We all looked at him confused.

"That we've seen the last of Jerry rations," he added. The room fell silent again.

"I'm goin' with we're gettin' outta this dump," Sidney said, breaking the silence.

"Me too," Willie said. "But I is gonna savor every last bite of that soup Roscoe's cookin'. That's foe sho'."

CHAPTER TWENTY-NINE

Extra! Read All About It!

January 26, 1945
Detroit, Michigan

"Dad… how did you meet mom?" I asked, as we drove to church.

"I bought 'er at Woolworth's," he replied from behind his cigar firmly clamped in the side of his mouth.

Mom shot him an icy stare.

"Just kiddin', my dear," he quickly said, placing his hand on hers. "Why ya ask, Doll-face?"

"Just wonderin'…" I answered.

Thinking of Jack made me wonder if they had ever faced a similar struggle.

"We took a boat ride together," Dad explained. "Well, not together. We just happened to be on it at the same time."

"The Bob-Lo boat?" I asked, referring to the pair of huge steamers that ferried passengers to Bois Blanc island, a small Canadian island south of Detroit in the Detroit River.

The island was famous for its amusement park and dance hall Henry Ford built there. Non-French speaking citizens couldn't pronounce the name correctly, and began to refer to it as "Bob-Lo" island, and the name stuck.

"No, Doll-face," my dad chuckled. "A much bigger boat. The RMS Olympic."

"Isn't that the big ocean liner I read about that hit and sunk a

German submarine in World War One?" I asked.

"One 'n the same, Doll-face. It was 1920, after the war, and she had just been converted back to civilian use. Your mother and her family were on the first voyage to America that she took. They were leaving Ireland for a new life in the U.S.," Dad explained. "I was seventeen years old and had lost my family and my home to the war. I happened to be on the same ship, pursuing the same dream," he told me.

"So the two of you fell instantly in love on the ship?" I asked, leaning forward and resting my arms on the back of the front seat.

My mom began to cackle.

"Well, I did. The moment I laid eyes on young Miss Anna Haddus," Dad explained. "But she felt otherwise."

"That's because you were a lowly tramp!" Mom laughed.

Dad gave her a look and puffed on his cigar.

"According to your father!" my dad bellowed. "But I kept at it."

"That's right," mom said, wrapping her arms around his right arm. "But you have to admit, you sort of had us held captive on that ship for fifteen days. You wore us both down though. You're my tramp now," she cooed at him.

My dad turned the corner leading onto Radnor Street, and past my dream house. The For Sale sign was long gone, yet no one had moved in yet.

"I sure wish Jack and I could have gotten that house," I sighed. "I wonder who bought it anyway? They sure don't seem to be in any hurry to move in," I added, watching the house go past.

My mom still had her left arm under my dad's arm. She looked at him with a loving smile and gently tapped on his arm with her right hand. He stared straight ahead and drove on, puffing on his cigar.

"I'm sure the two of you will find a home you both love," she told me.

"I know," I lamented.

I looked at the both of them and thought about their story. They not only dealt with the inconveniences of a war, they survived one. They left Ireland with nothing to start from scratch in a whole new place. How ironic it was they sailed on a ship that was famous for sinking a German submarine. I chuckled to myself while I thought of how my dad had to win over her dad, just like Jack had to do with him.

I looked at Mom smiling at Dad, and caught a brief glimpse of him smiling back, albeit staring straight ahead, rather than at her. It all seemed to have worked out well for them. Their story had different circumstances, but wasn't all that different from ours. I wondered how Jack was doing. It did worry me that I hadn't heard anything in quite awhile.

"And now, the latest from Armed Forces Radio…" crackled over the car radio.

"Oh! Turn that up!" I shouted.

My dad turned the volume up a bit.

"It has been reported that as of today, Soviet troops have liberated Nazi concentration camps at Auschwitz… I repeat Soviet troops have taken over and liberated Nazi concentration camps at Auschwitz. This news comes on the heels of the end of the Battle of the Bulge on January 16, and the capture of the city of Warsaw, Poland, also under Soviet control since January 17, marking continued progress for the Allies against the Nazi Regime."

"Oh! That is wonderful news!" I squealed, sitting back in the seat next to my sisters.

"President Roosevelt is preparing to meet with Churchill and Stalin to discuss further actions to be taken in the war, terms of a German surrender, and redistribution of occupied territories. This has been a report of Armed Forces Radio… we now return you to your regular programming."

I beamed with pride and anticipation. A German surrender? Could the war be finally coming to a close?

I wondered how close troops were to liberating where Jack was. I imagined the map I had hung in my bedroom and the progress I had been marking on it. The liberating of Auschwitz meant the Soviets had reached the western border.

The Allies had already crossed the eastern border. Jack was right in the middle of it all. If I could only hear from him, and know he was okay.

My dad turned the car into the church parking lot and squeaked to a stop.

I went into the church with all the hope I could muster that soon this would be over, and Jack would soon be home.

I had some serious praying to do!

CHAPTER THIRTY

C'mon Uncle Joe!

February 14, 1944
Stalug Luft One
Barth, Germany

I lit up the last cigarette in my last pack and stood in the cold, staring at a big empty spot where there should be a wagon full of potatoes. I'd settle to see a pile of them, but there wasn't a single potato to be seen. I let out a ragged sigh. I didn't think I could feel any hungrier than I already was. Turns out I was wrong.

"You seen Lucky anywhere?" I heard a voice behind me say.

"Huh?" I said, turning to see Leon standing behind me.

"Lucky," he told me. "Have ya seen 'em? I dunno where that cat has gotten to…"

"Naw. I ain't seen 'em," I told Leon. "Prb'y hidin' somewhere, with all the sirens been goin' off the past few days," I suggested.

"Yeah, but he usually comes back once they are done… where the hell's the potato pile?" Leon asked, noticing the lack thereof.

"Beats me," I responded, taking a drag off my cigarette.

"Well, hell!" Leon shouted. "They better give us something. We ain't got nothin' left!"

My stomach complained loudly.

"Maybe there's bread," I said.

Leon lit up a cigarette and we both started walking to the north compound where the bread cart was.

"It sure is cold out!" Leon grumbled, pulling up his collar to ward off the stiff wind howling in off of the Baltic.

177

I pulled mine up and zipped my jacket all the way up to the neck.

"I know. An' I'm losin' all the fat I had to keep me warm," I answered.

We entered the north compound and rounded the corner of the barracks to see the bread cart stacked with bread in the middle of the compound.

"Nur ein Brot!" one of the guards standing next to it told us.

"Well, one loaf is better'n nothin'," Leon said. "When are we getting potatoes?" he asked the guard.

The guard looked at him as if he didn't understand.

"Wann werden wir Kartoffeln bekommen?" Leon asked him.

"Keine Kartoffeln," he responded.

"What'd he say?" I asked Leon.

"Not to hold our breath waitin'."

We each took a loaf of bread and started to walk back to our barracks.

"Es gibt Karroten!" the guard stated, pointing to a heaping pile of carrots behind the bread wagon. "Sie machen nehmen funf."

We went back and took five carrots each from a small pile.

"Guess it's something," I said

Just then I felt the ground begin to shake. I heard a loud roar approaching that sounded like an airplane.

VAARROOOOOMMMMM!! A P-38 roared right over our heads, and I instinctively ducked. Another one flew over a minute later, setting off the air raid sirens.

"What the hell??" Leon shouted over the commotion as we ran back to our barrack.

As the pair streaked off to the east, I looked up and noticed USAAF insignias on them. The pilot in one of them tipped his wings to say hello.

We reached our barracks and ran inside, slamming the door behind us.

"What the hell was that?!" Roscoe yelled.

We stood there out of breath for a second.

"It was two P-38's!" I shouted. "They were OURS!"

"What the hell are P-38's doin' here?!" Joe asked.

"Are you sure it was 38's?" Robert asked.

"What the hell else kind of plane is quiet til it's right on top of ya and has two tails?!" I shouted.

"The Army quit usin' 'em for combat in Europe last year. They were too slow, compared to the new Messerschmidts. It's all P-51's now," he explained.

"But I saw 'em clear as day, and I'm tellin' ya, they were 38's," I said. "Nothing else in the Air Force has that distinctive double tail."

"They quit usin' 'em for combat… but they still use 'em… for reconnaissance," he explained. "They weren't here to fight. They were here to see what lies ahead."

That was a very good sign. It meant Allied troops were getting close. A wonderful smell filtered through my nostrils as I set the loaf of bread and carrots down on the table.

"Hey! Bring 'dem carrots over here!" Roscoe said. "It's jus' what I needed!"

I turned to see him standing at the stove in front of a steaming pot. That was where the smell was coming from.

"What's cookin'?" Leon asked. "It smells damn good."

"I caught a rabbit," Roscoe answered him.

"Where the hell did you find a rabbit?" I asked. "We've been havin' a hard time seein' rats, let alone a rabbit," I added, carrying some carrots over to him.

"Who cares!" Joe scoffed. "We get to eat. That's all that matters."

That was true. I couldn't remember the last time we ate anything. Prisoners were resorting to eating anything they could find. Some had starved to death. Every day, there were more fresh digs in the makeshift graveyard near the garden area on the north end of the compound. How Roscoe managed to find and catch a rabbit was beyond me, but it was certainly a gift from God, as were the P-38's that just flew over us.

"The Pow-Wow had more good news," Joe told us.

"What did it say?" I asked.

"Roosevelt, Churchill, and Stalin had a Pow-Wow of their own to draft the terms for a German surrender. Two days later Dresden went up in flames. Bombed right to the damn ground," he responded.

Yet another important target had been hit hard. Allies were already meeting to discuss German surrender. Reconnaissance flights had marked our position, and we finally had something to eat cooking on the stove.

"Looks like our luck has taken a turn for the good today," I said.

"Hey, that reminds me!" Leon said. "Any of you guys seen Lucky? I've been lookin' all over hell for that damn cat, and can't find him anywhere."

Roscoe whistled a happy tune as he stirred the pot and smiled.

"I'm sure he'll turn up... somewhere. Prb'y where you'd least expect him," he said.

"You're probably right. He is a tough ole cat..." Leon said.

Roscoe continued to stir. He poked at the carcass in the pot.

"Let's hope not," he muttered quietly.

CHAPTER THIRTY-ONE

The Right Thing to Do

March 16, 1945
Stalug Luft One
Barth, Germany

"So, what was that all about?" Joe asked Robert as he came through the door.

Robert went straight to the table and sat down with a somber look on his face. Since Robert had been here the longest and held the rank of lieutenant when he went down, we appointed him as the leader of our barrack. He had just returned from what he had been told was a very important meeting with Col. Zemke, the highest ranking prisoner here and our liaison with the Germans.

"We all have a decision to make," Robert said.

We all gathered around him.

"About what?" Joe asked.

Robert shuffled his weight nervously. "We all know the war hasn't been goin' that well for the Krauts, right?" he asked.

"Yeah. Ain't been no bed 'a roses for us neither," Roscoe snorted.

"Well, here's the thing. Commandant Scherer and his officials had a meetin' with Zemke an' his staff," Robert explained. "They told Zemke that the Russians are closin' in on this place…"

"Whaa-hoo!!" Sidney yelled. "We're finally getting' outta here!"

"Not so fast, Sidney. It's complicated," Robert warned.

"How so?" Mike asked.

"The whole damn chain of Kraut command wants to scram before they get here… and they want us to come along," Robert said.

"Where they takin' us?" I asked.

"They didn't say," Robert said. "But we'd be doin' it on foot, likely someplace deep into Germany. Maybe even Berlin. They have no transportation. The train tracks are gone. There's only a few dilapidated old planes on that old runway south of camp. Not near enough to carry everyone. Same with trucks."

"So, what's this choice we have to make?" Willie asked.

"Zemke put his foot down when he was asked to ready everyone for the march, having heard of other marches that turned into death marches. He asked the Krauts if we could take a vote and see what we all thought," Robert said. "They approved it. We can go with the Krauts, or stay here and wait for the Russians and take our chances. Zemke agreed to take full responsibility for the prisoners in the camp if we stay."

"I say stay here!" Leon exclaimed. "Ain't the Russians our allies?"

"They are for now, but it's a strained relationship. With the war windin' down, the Allies are startin' to talk about redistributing the occupied territories, and Stalin wants to take Poland, lock, stock, and barrel. That ain't settin' well with Roosevelt and Churchill," Robert explained.

"We don't know how long it will take them to get here either. It could take months. By then, they could be our allies, or the enemy, it's hard to say," he explained. "We could starve to death if we stay. We would go from the meager rations the Krauts provide to fending for ourselves."

We had gotten Red Cross parcels a few days after the recon flights went over, but they were the first ones in months. We hadn't gotten any since either. The German rations might not have been plentiful, but it were something we could more or less count on.

"They've also learned that the first troops heading this way are actually Mongolian soldiers recruited by Stalin. Pretty bloodthirsty lot. They ride in on horses with swords and axes. They were the same ones that took Warsaw. The Russian troops that followed them in were held up by bad weather there. Modern tanks and trucks were stuck in deep snow, but it didn't even faze the Mongolians on horseback. By the time the Russians reached Warsaw and were able to rein 'em in, they had nearly killed everyone in sight," Robert told us. "What happens if they get here before the Russian troops?" he asked.

"Kinda damned if we do, damned if we don't..." Mike said.

"How soon we gotta decide?" Sidney asked.

"The Krauts aren't sure yet. They could be ready to bug in as soon as a week. But they have made it clear, if or when they do go, they'll do it with or without us. Zemke would like a decision within a few days," Robert reported.

I remembered the ten-mile walk I took when I went down. Berlin was roughly one hundred and seventy-five miles away, and likely where we would go. That seemed impossible in the malnourished state we were all in, and improbable if we were in perfect health. Staying sounded like the better option at first, but what would we do for food? What if strained relations between the Russians and Allies came to a boil? We could become Russian prisoners. Or, we could be killed by the Mongolian troops. Neither choice was an easy one. I needed time to decide.

"I'm gonna take a walk and think it over," I said, walking toward the door.

When I got outside, I stopped and lit a cigarette. The sky was clear and blue, and a nice, warm breeze was blowing. The warm sun felt good on my face while I walked along. It appeared that the cold winter weather was finally giving way to spring.

I reached the perimeter fence and began the same walk I'd taken around this place so many times. It had helped me pass time here. I'd used these walks to clear my head of memories of my crash. Not a day went by when I didn't have visions of Malloy being ripped from the plane, or of it slamming into the ground and exploding. I'd also used walks to help me with decisions like the one I had to make now.

"Ub-bub-bub-bub..." I heard someone say.

I rounded the corner of the compound and began to walk along the northern fence and noticed Cap'n Limey walking toward me. His gate was jerky and uneven. He was unshaven, disheveled, and filthy dirty. He had a blank, hollow, straight-ahead stare on his face. He had lost a lot of weight since I'd seen him last.

"Ub-bub-bub-bub..." he muttered to himself, not even noticing me as he step-shuffled past me.

It appeared that solitary and malnutrition had taken a heavy toll on him. I almost felt sorry for him.

I stopped at my favorite spot along the fence and listened to the soothing sound of the waves of the Baltic lapping against the shore. I looked over at the graveyard and saw three fresh mounds of dirt at the end of the rows of graves. I sure didn't want to end up there. I didn't want to be buried along the road to Berlin either.

I puffed on my cigarette and thought about the decision I had to make. We were so close to winning this war and going home I could taste it. Why did it have to come to this? Why couldn't we just be rescued? Why didn't these goddamn Krauts just stay and take it like men?

"'Allo, Meester Glite," I heard an unmistakeable voice say from behind me.

Now what? I turned around to see Benny standing there with an unlit cigarette between his fingers.

"Benny," I said, nodding to him.

He stood there with his cigarette still unlit, looking at me. I took out my lighter, lit it, and held it out. Benny held his cigarette in the flame, puffed on it, and let out a long sigh. He looked out at the waves lapping the shore.

"Zank you," he said. "It ees a beautiful day, ya?" he added.

"Not bad," I said, staring at the water in awkward silence. "What's on your mind?" I asked, expecting a series of questions regarding my whereabouts on a given day and time.

"Nothing-k," he answered. "I am zimply enjoyink da view."

"So I hear you're gonna turn tail an' run..." I said.

"Who tuld you zhis?" he asked.

"Your Commandant," I answered. "Afraid of gettin' a lil' roughed up is he?" I asked.

Benny took a long drag from his cigarette and smiled at me.

"He ees only conzerned for efferyone's zafety," Benny replied.

"Bein' safe ain't always best," I said, snuffing my cigarette out in the dirt. "Sometimes ya gotta do what's right instead."

"I agree!" Benny said. "Zat ees vhy I yam stayink right here!" he added.

"You're what?!" I asked.

"I yam stayink right here," Benny told me. "Zhis ees my home, zo zhis ees vhere I vill stay," he said, pointing at the ground.

"Won't you get in some sort of trouble?" I asked.

"It's poshible," Benny stated. "Und I could be in danger as vell. But I hauf made up my mind I vill not leave my home."

I had to admire Benny for his bravery. I stood silently with my hands in my jacket pockets looking out at the water and suddenly knew what my decision was. There really wasn't a good clear choice in the decision that had to be made; either one was dangerous. Staying was the right thing to do, no matter what happened. If the Commandant wanted to run, let him. I was staying right here where I was.

"I gotta hand it to ya Benny... you may be the enemy, but you know what's what."

"Vee are not enemies," Benny said pointing between us. "Our leaders are. Vee zimply hauf a job to do."

"You're too damn good at yours sometimes," I said and patted him on the back, not noticing the paper that had fallen from my jacket pocket.

"Vhat ees zhis?" Benny asked, stooping down to pick it up. It was a postcard to Eileen that I hadn't been able to send.

"A letter home perhaps?" Benny asked.

"Yeah," I said, sheepishly holding my hand out for it.

" I vill send it for you, eef you vould like," Benny told me.

"You'd do that… for me?" I asked.

"Auf course!" Benny responded. "Eet ees zee right zhing to do!"

Benny stuffed the postcard in his pocket and walked away.

I lit another cigarette and stared out at the Baltic.

"What was that about?" I heard Mike ask.

I turned to see him standing behind me, watching Benny walk away.

"You wouldn't believe me if I told ya," I said. "But, I've made up my mind. I'm stayin'."

"That makes it unanimous," Mike said.

"Huh?" I asked.

"I was comin' to tell ya," Mike said. "We all agree. We're not goin' anywhere. All of the prisoners in the whole damn place have told Zemke they are stayin' put. Hell, even the Krauts have decided to stay," he chuckled.

CHAPTER THIRTY-TWO

Last One Out, Turn Off the Lights

May 1st, 1944
Stalug Luft One
Barth, Germany

I opened my eyes and looked up at the bottom of the bunk above me.

"You hear that?" Willie asked me, sitting up in his bunk.

I listened carefully for the sound of planes or bombs in the distance, but I didn't hear a thing.

"I don't hear nothin'," I responded. My stomach rumbled loudly, "'cept that."

"Exactly!" Willie said.

One by one, Leon, Mike, and the others woke up. It had been a rough night for sleep. All night long we were seeing flashes of light and hearing bombs go off, some very close. I had heard gun shots off and on all night as well. I laid still and listened for any sounds outside. Nothing. Sidney and Robert got up and looked out the window.

"What 'cha see?" Roscoe asked. The pair tilted and twisted their heads around, taking in all they could see through the window.

"I don't see anybody," Sidney said.

"There's no guard in the tower either," Robert said, peering out at the tower to the south of our barrack.

"It's 0700," Leon said, looking at his watch. "Nobody rousted us for roll call?"

"What the hell is goin' on?" Joe asked.

We all got up and walked toward the door as a group. Robert slowly opened it a little and looked out. There wasn't a sound coming from the compound. Robert opened the door all the way and we walked outside. The place resembled a ghost town. I didn't see anyone. There weren't any other prisoners to be seen anywhere. I looked in each guard tower, and noticed that not a single one was manned. Not a single guard was patrolling the compound. An eerie silence was all there was.

Slowly, more and more prisoners peeked out of their barracks, eventually coming out to the empty compound.

"What the hell?" Joe asked.

"Look!" Robert said, pointing to the wide open gate leading into the prison. We walked to the center of the compound where we could see more gates. All of them were hanging wide open. More groups of prisoner wandered out and joined us. It was kind of surreal. Where the hell were all the Germans?

"I'm gonna go find Zemke. Stay inside the compound til I get back," Robert said.

He began to run toward the north compound.

"What's goin' on?" some of the other prisoners asked us.

"Wo dunno," Sidney told them, "Anybody seen any guards around?" he asked the gathering crowd.

Everyone shook their heads no. We all walked over and stared at the wide open gate. Robert ran back and joined us.

"The Germans left last night," he told the crowd. "Col. Zemke has taken control of the camp."

"So… are we free?" a prisoner asked.

Robert shrugged his shoulders.

"In a sense, yes," Robert told him. "Col. Zemke strongly suggests you stay here until it can be determined what will happen. If you would like to explore the town, you are free to do so, but be warned, we have no idea who, or what, is out there. If you go out of the compound, be very careful. Any information you can gather out there is helpful. All prisoners are to be back inside the compound by 1600 hours."

"What if we want to leave on our own?" another prisoner shouted from the back.

"You will not be punished if you decide to strike out on your own, but I wouldn't suggest it since we know so little about who controls the territory at this time," he answered.

The crowd began to disperse and Robert rejoined our group.

"I'd like all of you to pair up and do some exploring," Robert told us.

"Who the hell came through here last night?" Joe asked.

"All evidence suggests the Mongolian troops. All Zemke knows is Scherer called him in last night and told him he and his staff was leaving," Robert told us.

"They still around?" Sidney asked.

"That's what we need to find out," Robert said. "Seems odd we haven't seen anyone yet. I would think if it were regular troops, this would be a high-priority place to visit and secure. Mike and Jack, go to the outlying area around the sea. Leon and Willie, cover the north end of town. Sidney and Roscoe, you search the west end. Joe, you and I will do the east side. Everyone make yourself invisible and see what you can find out about who is in control of the area. We'll meet back here at 1600 to see what we've found," he instructed us.

Mike and I set out for the gate facing the Baltic on the north side of the compound. I stopped before going through the open gate and stared at the fence.

"Feels like we're doin' something wrong, doesn't it?" I asked Mike.

"Kind of," Mike chuckled. "But in a good way," he added while we walked toward the roads and large homes along the shoreline.

It was odd to not see a single person out and about. Normally during the day there was some activity, but today it was dead quiet.

"Mike…" I said, holding my arm out and stopping him.

"What?" He asked.

"Look," I said, pointing at the front door of the first house we came to.

It was hanging wide open. We walked slowly to the front of the house and peered in the windows. Lights were still on inside the house. I didn't see anyone.

We slowly and quietly went inside the house. I could hear a methodical click-click-click sound coming from the living room. When I eased into the doorway of the living room, I noticed a phonograph still running. The needle was at the end of the record, making the clicking sound.

"Somebody left here in a hell of a hurry," I said.

Mike entered the room, took the needle off of the record and shut the phonograph off.

"Anybody home?" he shouted. There was no answer. "Hello! We mean no harm!" he said.

The house was silent. We went from room to room and found no one.

"Well, lookie here…" Mike said, entering the kitchen.

Hanging on the wall were several huge homemade sausages and knackwurst. Mike took a knife from the counter and cut them down, then slid the knife into the inside pocket of his jacket.

We went back outside and I noticed two sets of footprints in the sand on the shore across the road. They led to water and a mark in the sand that looked as if something big and heavy had been dragged into the water. Along the shore there were small row boats dotting the beach in front of every house, except this one.

"Looks like they headed out to sea," I said.

"In a hell of a hurry too… look how far apart the steps are," Mike noticed. "They were running to that boat."

We continued on to the next house, noticing the front door was also open, and the huge window facing the sea was shattered. Mike walked up and looked inside the window.

"Aww, shit!" he said, holding his hand over his mouth.

He ran from the house and fell to his knees in the yard and began to throw up.

I went to the window and looked in. A young woman's body was lying in a pool of blood on the floor. Her skirt had been removed and she was laying spread eagle, naked from the waist down. Her throat had been cut so deep, she was nearly decapitated.

I entered the house and found the body of a young man shackled to the wall in the kitchen. He was covered in blood and had been stabbed with something very large several times.

I slowly made my way to a bedroom, and found a suitcase lying on the bed. Dresser drawers were hanging open and clothes were tossed into the suitcase and all over the bed. A large ornate wooden box with intricate carvings sat at the foot of the bed.

"Looks like they were tryin' to get away," Mike said entering the room.

I opened the box and found several stacks of different types of currency from several different countries.

"Holy shit!" Mike exclaimed. "That's a lotta loot!"

"Yeah, and from the looks of it, they ain't gonna be usin' it anytime soon," I said, stuffing my pockets.

I didn't know how or if we'd get out of Barth, but if need be, we'd have the funds to get the hell out of here on our own.

We went back outside and continued on the road that followed the shore and around the eastern side of town.

"Look!" Mike said, kneeling down and pointing at the gravel road.

Two sets of horse tracks ran down the center of the road. They were huge tracks, likely from draft horses pulling a large wagon. But there were no wheel tracks. We followed the tracks around a curve and slight rise in the road and noticed a body laying face down in the distance.

When we got closer, I noticed the body was wearing a German soldier's uniform. He was tall and lanky looking, with huge boots on his feet. His pants appeared way too short.

"No," I muttered, running toward the body. "No, No, NO! Dammit!" I yelled, turning the body face up.

It was Benny, and it appeared he had been stabbed and dragged down the road face down.

"Sons of bitches," I seethed.

"Poor Benny," Mike said. "What a way to go."

"We can't just leave him here," I said, grabbing Benny's body under his arms. "Gimme a hand, would 'ja?" Mike sighed, stuffed the sausages inside his jacket and grabbed Benny by the feet.

"Think he'd do this for you?" Mike asked me as we lugged the body back to camp.

"Yes... I really think he would," I grunted.

"I dunno," Mike said. "He sure watched you like a hawk."

"He was just doin' his job," I wheezed, "He actually was a damn good guy, considerin' "

A horse's whinny stopped us both in our tracks.

We turned and found ourselves face to chest with the biggest horse I had ever seen. Mounted on top of the monstrous jet black horse was a huge bearded man glaring at us. He was wearing pants, boots, and a long coat made of animal hide with dark brown fur. He had a metal helmet with a huge spike on the top and a nose guard that extended down the front between his eyes. A large machete hung from a sheath around the horses neck. He was holding a huge jousting stick that was covered in blood in his right hand.

We stood there dumbfounded while he stared at us with eyes as black as coal. He lowered his jousting stick and pointed it at both of us, then toward the prison camp, grunting at us. When we didn't move, he gave us an angry stare and shook his stick toward the camp.

"We're goin!" Mike told him while we scrambled to pick Benny up.

"Het!" he shouted and pointed the jousting stick at Mike.

He moved his horse closer slowly inching the stick toward Mike's chest. Mike was trembling. He dropped Benny's feet and held his hands up, but the bloody stick kept slowly heading toward him, eventually spearing a large sausage that was sticking out of the top of his jacket.

The soldier pulled the sausage from Mike's coat, brought it up to himself, took it off the stick, and placed it in his saddlebag.

Then he grunted at us, smiled, and rode away.

The War is OVER!

May 7, 1945
Detroit, Michigan

"This is gonna look beee-autiful on your dress!" Dot exclaimed, holding up a strip of white lace with small pearlescent teardrops weaved into it.

"Yeah!" Let's get enough for your veil too!" Doe's voice echoed through Hudson's Department Store.

My sisters and I were getting the last of the material for my wedding dress so it could be ready when Jack finally did come home.

"May I help you?" the clerk asked.

"Yes. I'd like... three yards of this," I told her, handing her the strip of lace.

"I'd get four," Rosie said, "It's something we can use if there are leftovers."

"Four it is then," I told the clerk.

While she cut and packaged the lace I thought of Jack. I had finally gotten a note from him letting me know he was okay and that there had been a problem with getting mail in or out. For the longest time it seemed this war had been going three steps forward and two steps back, but the news has been very promising lately. World leaders had been trying to get Germany to surrender, and while nothing was certain, it appeared the end could be near.

"That will be thirty-nine cents, Miss," the clerk told me. "This is beautiful... what are you making with it, may I ask?" she added.

"We're makin' her wedding dress!" Dot beamed, pointing at me.

"Oh my! Congratulations!" the clerk told me. "When's the lucky day?"

"I can't really say for sure," I answered. "My man is a prisoner of war in Germany right now, but I will be ready when he gets home," I told her, handing her the money for the lace.

"You keep that," she said, folding my hand back over the change. "And you tell that man of yours that I am proud of him!"

"Gee! Thanks!" I told her.

My sisters and I walked out of the store and toward the corner to wait under the Kern's clock for the bus to arrive.

I couldn't have asked for nicer weather. There wasn't a cloud in the sky and a gentle warm breeze circled around the tall buildings. I stood under the clock and enjoyed the feeling of the warm sun on my face. I was looking forward to spring.

"When Johnny comes marching home again, Hurrah! Hurrah! We'll give em a hearty welcome then Hurrah! Hurrah!" echoed from the radio speaker on the front of Kern's Department Store. My sisters and I smiled at each other.

"The men will cheer an' the boys will shout! The ladies they will all turn out! And we'll all feel gay when Johnny come marching hooome!!" we harmonized along with the song. We locked our arms together and began to sing loudly, not caring what the crowd on the corner thought of us.

"The old church bell will peel with joy Hurrah! Hurrah! To welcome home our darling boy Hur..."

"THIS JUST IN!" the radio announcer bellowed, interrupting the song.

We stopped singing and everyone standing on the corner listened.

"Sources have confirmed that Adolph Hitler has committed suicide! I repeat! Sources have now confirmed the death of Nazi leader, Adolph Hitler, who has committed suicide! We have also just learned that General Alfred Johl, Chief of Operations Staff in the German High Command, as well as Admiral Von Freideburg of the German Navy and Major Wilhelm Oxenius of the German General Staff, have all just signed a document of unconditional German surrender at General Eisenhower's Headquarters in Reims, France! The war in Europe is over, folks! I repeat! The war in Europe is OVERRRR!!"

The entire corner erupted in loud cheers. Hats were flying everywhere, horns were honking, and people began to dance in the street

"The war is over?!" I gasped.

I looked at my sisters who were staring wide-eyed and open-mouthed back at me. The war is over. The war... is... over. It began to sink in. It was really over! Tears streamed down my cheeks and my package dropped at my feet.

"The war is over!!" my sisters shouted in unison, taking me by my hands.

"The war is over!!" we all shouted, jumping up and down. I began to cry like a baby.

"THE WAR IS OVER! THE WAR IS OVER!! THE WAR IS OVER!!!!!

CHAPTER THIRTY-FOUR

Need a Lift, Buddy?

May 12, 1944
Stalug Luft One
Barth, Germany

"Pack your bags, my friends!" Robert said, entering our barrack. "We're outta here!"

"Say what?!" Willie asked.

"I thought the Russians were takin' us the scenic route in a coupla days?" Sidney asked.

"Zemke just got off the horn with General Gross, commander of the First Air Division. Seems he talked the Russians into lettin' him get us out!" Robert said. "But they only gave 'em two days, so we need to pack it up now. They will be arriving within the hour!"

"We don't have to go through Russia and all that shit?" Joe asked.

"The General nixed that idea. We're not going home by slow train through Russia, we're goin' home by plane today," Robert explained.

"What do the Russians think of that idea?" Roscoe asked.

"They ain't happy about it, but the good General has told 'em, and I quote 'If ya don't like it, tough shit'," Robert explained. "We're finally goin' home men," he sighed.

I couldn't believe my ears. It was finally happening. The past two weeks had been strange, to say the least. Russian troops eventually rolled into Barth to relieve the Mongolians, but tensions between the Allies and Russia had left us in the middle. We hadn't really been prisoners, but we weren't free either, while the two sides argued about how we would be released. Yesterday, we had been told the Russians were going to take us by train in a few days to Odessa, a port on the Black Sea, deep inside Russia. From there we would slowly work our way back to England and the U.S. None of us liked the idea; we wanted to go home. To me, it felt like a stall tactic to get us into Russia and hold us as pawns to get what they wanted out of this war, that being all of Poland.

"They want us packed and ready to go by 1000 hours. Get outside and gather in groups of 25-30 men and line up at the airstrip just south of town. It's a very time-critical mission, so be ready!" Robert instructed us.

"I can't believe this happening!" Mike told me as we both gathered up our things and tossed 'em in our suitcases. "Pinch me, would'ja? I wanna make sure this ain't a dream."

"I know!" I told him. "Havin' a hard time believin' it myself. But I ain't complainin'. Just get me the hell outta here."

We finished packing and walked outside to a flurry of activity. Sick and injured prisoners were being loaded into trucks and driven to the airstrip. A single-file row of prisoners able to walk snaked out of the compound toward the airstrip.

I lit a cigarette and looked around the camp, thinking of all I'd lived through in my time here. As I walked to the airstrip, everything I had gone through played through my mind like a silent movie.

There were fun times with Mike, training back in the States. One by one, I remembered my crew. Visions of LaFlame, Levine, Austin, T.C., Ortlip, J.J., Malloy, and Rocky smiling and joking around passed through my mind. I remembered how nervous we all were the first time we flew in combat. I thought of that harrowing mission we barely made it back from. I saw the Purple Heart slam into the ground and explode. I remembered Malloy. I thought about O'Neil volunteering to fill in for Rocky, not knowing what lay ahead for him. I pictured his family anxiously awaiting his return, then learning he wouldn't be coming home after all. The farmer who was holding that pitchfork in my face, looking just as scared as I was, and the S.S. Officer standing over me filtered through my mind.

Visions of the ten-mile walk, the train rides, Pickhardt and his dogs, and seeing what they did to Willie played on in a slow motion movie I'd seen too many times already. I remembered recognizing Mike and could almost smell the burned flesh again.

I saw the Mongolian picking the sausage from Mike's coat with a bloody lance. I saw Benny and his goofy demeanor. I saw him lying dead in the streets of Barth.

"You're awful quiet..." Willie told me as we walked along.

"Just thinkin' about all we've been through," I said.

"I've been doin' the same," he said. "I dunno how, but we made it."

"It was lessons learned in the school of hard knocks," I reasoned. "I had a pretty rough row to hoe all my life. Funny thing is, I don't think I'd have survived this if I hadn't."

"You may be right," Willie laughed.

In the distance, I heard the sound of airplanes getting closer. The engines had a familiar roar to them. I shielded my eyes from the sun and scanned the sky for the planes. Silhouetted in the sun, I caught a glimpse of the big four-engine planes coming in.

I couldn't believe my eyes. It was a squadron of B-17's. A smile came across my weary face.

FORTRESSES. At least thirty of them. I chuckled as I watched them roar over us, circle the camp, and come in for a landing. I started the war flying in a Fortress, only to wind up in this fortress. I didn't know if I'd ever leave here mentally, but physically, I'd be doing it in yet another Fortress. How appropriate!

The planes landed, yet never stopped moving as prisoners ran up and piled into them. The planes then turned and took off again. Before we knew it, we were standing at the open door of our own flight.

We climbed in the plane and I noticed all of the guns and ball turret had been removed. In their place were plywood floors, making room for more passengers.

I followed the prisoners ahead of me, and eventually sat shoulder-to-shoulder on the floor of the radio room with Mike, Willie, and my roommates from Barth. I looked up at the radio operator smiling back at us.

"You're goin' home!" he shouted over the roar of the engines.

We all looked at each other and laughed. It really was happening. Home was just over the horizon.

The engines roared and the plane moved swiftly down the runway. The wheels left the ground and we climbed into the air, circling the camp. I looked out the window at the rows of shallow graves in the edge of the garden. A sad smile came over my face as I looked at the freshest one with Benny's boots and helmet on top of it. I watched Stalug Luft One slowly get smaller and eventually disappear.

I leaned back against the wall of the plane and tried to stop the never-ending visions of my experiences play through my mind again. The words I had read in solitary crossed my mind, so I opened my suitcase, took my journal out and wrote,

I'm sitting here thinking of things I left behind.
And it's hard to put on paper what's
goin' through my mind.
I've flown a batch of airplanes over a
hell of a patch of ground
A drearier place this side of hell,
is waiting to be found.
But there's one consolation, sit closer while I tell
When I die, I'll go to Heaven,
for I've done my hitch in Hell.

Epilogue

By flying non-stop, the crews of thirty modified B-17's evacuated all American and British prisoners at Stalug Luft One in the allotted 48 hours. Original calculations were at 130 pounds a man, each plane would be capable of carrying 25-30 men. When the evacuation began, it was found that the average weight of the prisoners at Stalug Luft One was closer to 90 pounds and each plane was able to carry as many as 35 men. British prisoners were taken directly to England, and American prisoners were taken to Camp Lucky Strike in LeHavre, France for treatment for malnutrition, dysentery, diphtheria, and pellagra.

When flights back home to the States were delayed, all American prisoners were given a choice to wait, or take a ride home by ship. Most gladly accepted the ride by ship. Jack, Mike, Leon, Joe, Robert, Roscoe, Sidney, and Willie exchanged addresses and vowed to keep in touch. Efforts were made, but it never happened.

Jack arrived in Detroit on June 5th, 1945. He and Eileen were married June 6th and began their life together. Mike Postek was Jack's best man.

At the reception, Jim Shea got his new son-in-law aside, and told him that he knew the man who bought the house on Radnor Street, and he was interested in selling it. When Jack inquired further, Jim gave him the deed, and told him the house would cost him "one dollar... and not a penny less."

Jack was offered a pay raise from $25.08 to $32.56 a week to re-enlist. What he told them is not printable here. Instead, he took a job working at Gratiot Lumber and insulated houses on the side.

Willie Strong returned to Detroit and also got a job at Gratiot Lumber. He worked for Jack in the insulation business as well.

Mike Postek returned to Pittsburg to learn his parents were killed in a car crash the day before he arrived. After the funeral, he accompanied his older sister back to her home in Ft. Myers, Florida and wound up staying there. He was an American Airlines pilot for twenty years. When the jet age arrived, he began to miss the old prop planes, so he retired and flew Pan-Am Clippers between Florida and the Caribbean.

Sidney Porter went back to Mt. Vernon, Illinois, and had that steak and glass of milk at the Whistle Stop, where he fell head over heels in love with his waitress, Pearl. Local entrepreneur and car dealer Virgil Bailey struck up a conversation with Sidney while at the diner that day. To show his appreciation for Sidney's service, he paid for the meal and gave him a job selling new Hudson's at his dealership on Tenth Street.

Roscoe Hayes went back to Charleston, Indiana, and opened a diner of his own which turned out to be a huge success. His signature dishes were so popular in the area, he eventually built a large upscale restaurant/nightclub that quickly became the place to go. He named the place Lucky's. Cat was not on the menu.

Joe Caparosa and Robert Plude decided to stay in the military and enjoy a cushy stateside duty flying B-24's from town to town, selling war bonds and talking about their experiences in the war. When that tour was over, Joe trained new recruits in the art of survival. Robert retired from the military, bought an Army surplus Curtiss Wright CW-22 Falcon, and worked as a crop duster in Kileen, Texas, not far from Hondo, where he learned to fly.

Leon Swisher went back to his home in the mountains of south central Pennsylvania and was never heard from again.

Harold "Kid" Ortlip was the only other survivor from the wreckage of The Purple Heart. The entire crew of the other unnamed

B-17 involved in the crash was lost as well. It was their first mission.

Jesus "Rocky" Rodriguez recovered from his surgery, was assigned to a new crew, and flew two more missions. He was KIA when his plane went down over Berlin.

Lt. Col. Reginald Archibald III, a.k.a., "Cap'n Limey," was spotted wandering out of the Stalug Luft One on May 1st, muttering to himself. He was never seen or heard from again.

On February 6th, 1945, Captain Pickhardt initiated the 1735 mile long Black March from Stalug Luft Four in Greater Tychow, Poland. Prisoners were forced to march 15-20 miles a day in extremely harsh conditions. They arrived at Stalug Luft 357 near Fallingbostel, Germany on April 3rd, 1945. During the march, Pickhardt was subdued by his own troops and turned over to the Allies. He hung himself in his jail cell awaiting trial for inhumane treatment of prisoners.

The mysterious man with a German accent who was following Eileen was injured in a freak accident when workers accidentally knocked some iron water pipes out a fourth floor window of the Book-Cadillac Hotel as he walked past. He was never seen after that.

Jim and Anna Shea watched the rest of their daughters get married and have children of their own. The pair enjoyed the company of their many grandchildren.

Jack Glide Sr. turned the insulation business over to Jack and enjoyed semi-retirement, helping out when needed. Jack, along with his dad and crew, finished the job on the Book-Cadillac, which led to more than a few awkward moments for the Blounts each time payday rolled around.

Jack and Eileen enjoyed thirty-seven happy years together. They raised five children and buried two, one died at birth, one was killed in a tragic car accident.

They eventually moved to northern Michigan where Jack managed a chain of lumber yards, and Eileen became a Magistrate Judge.

Jack eventually did get to see his paradise, when he and Eileen took a trip to Hawaii for their 35th wedding anniversary.

Eileen passed away in 1981 after a long bout with cancer.

Jack was reunited with her and rejoined the crew of the Purple Heart on Christmas Day, 2001.

Made in the USA
Charleston, SC
30 July 2013